RAY OF LIGHT

RAY OF LIGHT

THE HEALING PATH TO STEP OUT OF TRAUMA INTO JOY AND INNER PEACE

MARLENE MCCONNELL

NEW DEGREE PRESS
COPYRIGHT © 2022 MARLENE MCCONNELL
All rights reserved.
RAY OF LIGHT
The Healing Path to Step Out of Trauma Into Joy and Inner Peace

ISBN	979-8-88504-122-5	*Paperback*
	979-8-88504-752-4	*Kindle Ebook*
	979-8-88504-231-4	*Ebook*

To my loving family and friends,

Mamma, Daddy, my siblings, my niece, and my best friend.

This book is for you.

I also dedicate this book to all the angels that have touched my life, the ones in heaven and those walking the earth.

Lastly, to all the survivors.

You are a Ray of Light.

CONTENTS

	INTRODUCTION	11
CHAPTER 1.	HOW DID WE GET HERE?	19
CHAPTER 2.	TALK ABOUT IT	33
CHAPTER 3.	THE STRUGGLE TO DECIDE	49
CHAPTER 4.	GRIEF AND LOSS	65
CHAPTER 5.	RELIGION AND SPIRITUALITY	81
CHAPTER 6.	FORGIVENESS	97
CHAPTER 7.	COURAGE AND SURRENDER	111
CHAPTER 8.	THE VAGINA KEEPS THE SCORE	123
CHAPTER 9.	LIVING AUTHENTICALLY	139
CHAPTER 10.	STEPPING OUT OF TRAUMA	151
	ACKNOWLEDGMENTS	165
	APPENDIX	171

"None of us knows what might happen even the next minute, yet still we go forward. Because we trust. Because we have faith."

—PAULO COELHO

INTRODUCTION

"Trauma is not what happens to you; trauma is what happens inside you as a result of what happens to you."
—GABOR MATÉ

It is up to us to discover our ray of light in life. As a survivor of the dreaded disease cancer, sexual violence, attempted murder, divorce, grief, and loss, I've learned bad things can happen to anyone. However, I learned to become strong enough to restore my view of the world through these difficult circumstances, growing and finding my ray of light.

We can go from living our best lives to everything falling apart in a heartbeat. Without warning, we can find our entire lives turned upside down. The question is "How do we get through this?" and "Where do we start?"

On my life's healing journey, I found the path to step out of my trauma was not linear. The more people I met and engaged with, the more I learned I was not alone and we were all grappling with the same issues and similar circumstances. We were all connected in our search for a better life.

Unfortunately, I also learned that some people never tell their story, some try to never think about it, and some never seek the help they need.

It broke my heart to learn how many people suffered in silence with the shame of what happened to them. I lived with shame for a long time, and I learned that emotion makes your world very small, and you stop talking and connecting with people. The idea of people knowing is too much a thought to bear, so we retreat and disconnect from the world around us.

I want people to know they are not alone and they should not have to live with shame as a stigma. We often find that when we talk about it and shine a light on these hidden issues, it is not as bad as we thought it would be. People in this world have compassion and understanding for victims and survivors, and they treat them accordingly. So often, I hear beautiful stories of surprise when survivors open up and experience compassion for what they have gone through.

My healing journey started with a traditional methodology and psychology, and later it incorporated other modalities. I weaved talk therapy, religion, spirituality, and lived experiences together with self-love to empower me to choose to heal. The most essential and challenging part of the healing path was choosing to do so. In all my interactions with other survivors, they will always make a statement that confirms the power of choice. For many, making a decision is tough, and they have decision paralysis. They put plans in place but fail to follow through. All these things are normal.

Before choosing my healing path, I asked myself how badly I wanted to change. The answer was very badly, and I made the conscious decision to do the work required to heal. It was not glamorous, and there were many days and nights when I felt like giving up. I guess sometimes I did stray off the path, especially when it seemed like choosing the darkness was more accessible and more comfortable. After all, following my violent, traumatic experiences, it was easy to think, *What is my life worth anyway?* I could not even imagine anyone loving this broken, wounded girl. I believed all she was worthy of was being used.

When my thoughts were this dark, I questioned whether my life was worth living. Who wants to live with this doubt, pain, anger, disappointment, sadness, fear, and reminders of the past all of the time? It's like walking in a dark cave. Sometimes you are right at the back where it's very dark, and other times you get to go closer to the front where the ray of light is.

Just when I felt like giving up, I felt my intuition remind me I was wasting my life, a life that had value and purpose. I also experienced the affirmation through my intuition that my traumatic experiences were only a part of what informed my life's purpose. I want to say that by no means is it an easy task to choose to heal or to walk this path, but it's possible, and it starts with the willingness and the choice to do so.

The book brings to life my journey; for you, my reader, I hope it allows you to take what resonates and apply it in your own life. I start the book by understanding how we got here to this broken place, and I ask and answer whether there is hope to grow following trauma. Then, in each of the chapters that follow, I explore the path I took to heal each wounded part of me until I could step out of trauma to find freedom, joy, and inner peace in my life.

I take you through my darkest moments, and together we navigate the marshlands of despair. You can experience the healing progression and the lessons learned firsthand over the various chapters. We explored the different themes that I discovered on my path. All these themes are critical, and it starts with following our intuition. You can say intuition is how our subconscious mind communicates with the conscious mind. We are receiving essential information that our rational mind cannot access in this process. For example, we now know that "gut feeling" is real. Having that extra bit of knowledge readily available can considerably impact our choices in our lives.

I explore how we choose our lives and look at how others have done this. Some choices are easy, and some are difficult; some are not the best. Either way, life leads us and presents us with options, and if we pay attention, we will see it, and we can choose.

We can also choose to have faith and surrender to a Higher Power in our life. We don't have to wait for life to bring us to our knees, but we can do this consistently throughout our life through daily practice and starting small.

Whatever we take on as part of our healing comes back to making a choice. Through exercising choice in my life, I discovered a silver lining in the darkness, my ray of light. We sometimes forget we have a little light inside ourselves that lights up in the dark. When we feel we can't light our inner lamp, many people will shine their light so we can find our way. For example, after my diagnosis, my best friend shined her light by sitting with me and holding space for me so I could see beyond trauma and follow the illuminated path to joy and inner peace. When I was broken and bruised, it was my sister who helped me around the house, bathed me, fed me, clothed me, and sat with me even if it was in silence.

As much as I received light, I also shone my light for others through a smile, a word of encouragement, a shoulder to cry on, and sometimes presence when I did not have the words to soothe their pain.

Through my story and the stories of others in my book, I hope to empower, inspire, and educate you to know you are not alone. What happened to you is not your fault. There is a path that leads to joy and inner peace. Your experiences do not have to define you.

In life, we can be happy after trauma, but sometimes happiness requires self-reflection. However, when we experience joy, there is no doubt. It can be found in the simplest of things: a bright yellow house, a sunset, the laughter of a child.

Every person wants to have inner peace, peace in their hearts, minds, bodies, soul, homes, and relationships.

In today's world, everyone is talking about the collective trauma we all suffer because of COVID-19. For the first time, everyone on the planet understands the need to heal, take care of their mental health, and experience joy and inner peace. COVID-19 has allowed for much-needed global reflection and healing. This opened the door for more people to choose to live in the present, have greater self-awareness, and heal from trauma.

I believe we all react to trauma in different ways, experiencing a wide range of physical and emotional reactions. There is no "right" or "wrong" way to think, feel, or respond, so don't judge your reactions or those of other people. Your responses are normal reactions to abnormal events. It is essential to stay in the moment and move through coping, healing, and growth with grace.

I decided to write this book to share the accumulation of my life's experiences, knowledge, and wisdom within the world. In doing so, I tapped into my vulnerability to bring forth the most authentic and impactful version of my trauma recovery experience. I am writing this book for anyone who wants to choose a better life, find their voice, and become empowered to shine their ray of light.

Whatever the cause of your trauma, whether it happened years ago or yesterday, you can make healing changes and move forward with your life. But I always get asked, how? How do I step out of trauma? The answer is by being present in your mind, body, and soul; being an active participant in your life; and engaging with your life in a meaningful way. We can take what presents as the devastation that shattered our worldviews, and we can access a chance to learn to be present; feel our emotions; process our feelings; unlock healing and a deeper connection with the self, mind, body, and soul; and step out of trauma.

This book will appeal to you if you want to leave the struggle of past trauma behind. If you ask yourself, "How will I get through this?" or "Where do I start?" then this is the book for you.

If you are ready to step out of your trauma, then this is the book that will lead you to your ray of light.

CHAPTER ONE:

HOW DID WE GET HERE?

———

"Trauma is a fact of life. It does not, however, have to be a life sentence."

—PETER A. LEVINE

It was a hot summer Friday morning at the end of the season at the restaurant where I worked, and life was good. We had a meeting and planned out the last few shifts before the summer season officially ended. Before long, I would be back to university and settling into my daily routine. After the meeting, I said goodbye to my colleagues and headed out to the brand-new car my parents bought me for my birthday. Oh, how I loved that ride. I could do anything with time to kill, and I decided to chill at home before returning for my evening shift at the restaurant. As I got into my car, I turned up the music and enjoyed the summer breeze blowing through my hair. While I was driving, I started to feel like I should turn around and simply go back to the restaurant. These feelings were my intuition, raising the alarm, nudging me to change my plans. However, I actively powered through, not knowing what lay ahead for me.

What waited for me was not the chill afternoon I envisioned; instead, I came face to face with death. Shortly after entering the apartment, my nightmare began. I walked in and ran up the stairs to put my bag down. When I returned to the landing, I was grabbed from behind, my nose and mouth covered, and I could feel something pressed against my neck. My mind struggled to process what had happened. I remember thinking about who was playing this trick on me, but I soon realized this was no trick. A male voice whispered, "Who else is here?" but I could not find the words. "Walk," said the voice, and I took the first step to go down the stairs. Together we walked, and the man checked the kitchen, lounge, and dining room. As we passed the front door, I remember thinking the door could end this, but the door was locked, and even though the key was close, it was so very far away. I thought about grabbing the key, opening the door, and running, but the fear of potentially having my throat slit kept me from trying. As we turned around and headed back upstairs, all I could think about was the missed opportunity at the front door that I did not take. At that point, it felt like hours had passed since we came downstairs to clear the apartment. Not knowing what weapon was held to my neck, I complied with the demands.

I so badly wanted to scream, but there was no sound. Then, without warning, the violence began: the beating, the rape, the breaking of my bones, the attempt to dig out my eyes, the kicking, the slamming of my head into the wall and the floor, and ultimately the strangulation. Through it all, I fought with everything I had in me, and I was collecting evidence as I was going, semen, skin, saliva, everything I could take in those split seconds. Finally, the grip was so tight around my neck. It felt like trying to breathe through the eye of a small needle. In the last moments, as I gasped for air that was running out fast, I thought, *Don't let my niece come home and find my cold corpse*, and with that, I gave my last breath and collapsed into what I thought was my death.

While all this happened, the neighbors and passersby called the police. Two blocks from my apartment, a police captain doing his regular patrols received the call and responded swiftly. I would later come to know Captain van der Merwe as a man dedicated to his work in the police force, and that day he was committed to solving this case.

Back at the apartment, I was in a place that felt calm and peaceful. I started to see rays of beautiful yellow and orange light. I remember being drawn to all the beautiful colors. As the colors began to fade, the reality of where I was became apparent as I remembered in horror what had happened. The perpetrator ransacked my apartment and stole what he could while the accomplice kept a lookout. While trying not to breathe, move, or look alive, I could hear the sirens in the distance. This was the cue for him to leave. Not long after, there was a commotion coming up the stairs. I was so afraid because I thought, *He's coming back*. Next, I remember looking into the most beautiful blue eyes followed by a series of questions. The answers would send the captain and his team on a manhunt.

When it comes to surviving a traumatic event in life, we always choose to be a victim or a survivor, irrespective of what the trauma may be. Presented with this choice following my traumatic experience, I chose the road that led to becoming a survivor. When I am asked what the difference is between a victim and a survivor, I tell people the only time I was a victim was when it was recorded as such in the police docket. Being a survivor is a mindset, meaning I choose to live life despite what happened to me.

I am telling you this particular story of my life because I never believed something this horrific would ever happen to me. I grew up believing we are worthy of a well-meaning and kind world. I thought people were good, caring, and helpful and that we are prone to positive experiences rather than negative ones. However, having survived this traumatic, life-changing event, it shattered my view of the world and all the people in it. It impacted my life for years to come in a way that made me feel like the world was a cruel unsafe place and that nobody could be trusted. For a long time, this was my point of view, but not until I became intentional about my healing journey did I change that mindset and begin to experience post-traumatic growth. This led me to a place where I could interact with life in a meaningful way, step out of my trauma, and find joy.

Everyone hopes they will avoid the worst thing that life has to offer: accidents, illness, disease, loss, war, or violence in today's world. It is unfortunate to think how few of us will get through life unscathed. The World Mental Health Surveys 2017 of adults, carried out among seventy thousand participants from twenty-four countries, reported data that shows 70.4 percent of the respondents had experienced at least one type of traumatic event at some time in their life.

These findings clarify it is relatively likely to be exposed to very upsetting events in one's lifetime. Let's take a minute to think about our lives. We will find we either experienced a traumatic event ourselves or know at least one person who has experienced a traumatic event like the death of a loved one, an accident, or disease. If I think about my own life, I know at least twenty-five people who have experienced some type of traumatic event, and I encourage you to think about that in your life for a moment.

Of course, these traumatic events will inevitably cause great suffering, but I can tell you it is not all doom and gloom. As much as trauma can cause significant suffering in life, trauma can also be a powerful force for positive change. In my life, positive change happened over decades, and I learned everything I did following the trauma to support my choice to live life had a positive influence. For example, I attended many therapy sessions with my psychologist, and as a result, I came to have a better understanding of who I was, what was important in life, and how to identify, feel, and process my feelings and emotions. As a result, I grew emotionally over time. At the same time, my need to search for the meaning of life after trauma led me closer to God, which helped me grow spiritually. Attending sessions with a sexologist helped me understand my sexuality, desires, what I like and don't like, and what intimacy means to me. Everything that I did to support my choice to live started to restore my worldview and grow as a human being, physically, emotionally, spiritually, and mentally.

The following theory helped me understand why my worldview changed so drastically following trauma. In 1992, psychologist Dr. Ronnie Janoff-Bulman described the theory of shattered assumptions in her book, *Shattered Assumptions: Towards a New Psychology of Trauma*. This theory helped explain the adjustment after a traumatic experience that challenges a person's belief system or worldview. This made sense because my view of the world had been shattered, and I had difficulty making sense of it.

In a nutshell, the theory of shattered assumptions states that people operate according to a conceptual system based on assumptions about the world, the self, and others. These personally held assumptions help us make sense of the world and our role in it. They also allow us to feel safe, capable, and in control of what happens to us and those around us. Psychologists refer to our basic assumptions as the "assumptive world." Experts believe significant distress and disruption can occur when extreme events challenge this assumptive world (Janoff-Bulman, 1992).

Ronnie Janoff-Bulman discusses three main assumptions that trauma can challenge through the theory of shattered assumptions.

Benevolence of the World

In general, people believe the world is a good place, or rather their world is a good place.

The belief in benevolence entails the assumption that people are generally good, caring, and helpful and events are predominantly positive rather than negative in the outcome. Secondly, we distinguish between the world in general and the world we live in. The people and events that touch us constitute our world, and we expect these people and events to be benevolent rather than malevolent (Snyder, 1999). If we believe these assumptions, it may create a situation in which we underestimate the likelihood that adverse experiences may penetrate our lives. So, it comes as a significant surprise when it happens, and it shatters our view of the world, leaving us feeling hopeless and helpless in an unfamiliar world.

Meaningfulness of the World

The meaningfulness assumption refers to beliefs that the world is orderly, just, and logical. In other words, the assumption is that the distribution of good and bad outcomes makes sense. We believe there is no misfortune but a meaningful relationship between people and what happens to them. When we invoke this just assumption, we might think we have more control over events than we do, perceiving the outcomes as deserved. This assumption also allows us to minimize the randomness in our lives.

The question following the shattered view is, "Why?" as in, "Why did this happen to me?" or, "Why not me?" As we search for meaning, we may blame ourselves or someone else for the trauma. Yet, as hectic as that may feel, it may feel even worse to struggle with the possibility that bad things happen randomly.

Self-worth

The third assumption in our inner world is self-worth: the belief that we are good, decent, competent people. We regard ourselves as good because we can focus on the positive aspects of ourselves. When it comes to justice, we see ourselves as people who deserve good things, and, regarding control, we see ourselves as people who engage in the right behaviors. Our self-worth then provides us further support for believing in our comfort and security. Through this assumption, we live life from the perspective that bad things can happen, but with a sense of certainty that they will not happen to us. This assumption is shattered following a traumatic event, and it leads to a person questioning their sense of self and saying, "I never thought this could happen to me"(Janoff-Bulman, 1992).

I believed the world was a good, orderly, just, and logical place and that I was a person deserving of good things. After surviving the attack at my apartment, I struggled to reconcile this worldview with the traumatic event, and, with my basic assumptions shattered, I was forced to confront my vulnerability and face my fragility. In the years that followed, I embarked on a journey to rebuild my shattered assumptions, heal my life, and grow posttrauma.

An essential part of my overall healing journey is the willingness to be open to posttraumatic growth. In the 1980s, two psychologists, Richard Tedeschi and Lawrence Calhoun, from the University of North Carolina at Charlotte conducted research into the emerging field of the psychological study of post-traumatic growth. According to the 2015 "How trauma can change you for the better" article in *Time*, their findings reflected that trauma could bring a fundamental positive change in people in over 50 percent of cases. They also found that posttraumatic growth showed how the suffering caused by traumatic experiences could be channeled as a force for self-improvement rather than destruction. Following traumatic events, not all the changes were negative, but what was surprising for them was most of the trauma survivors interviewed for their research had reported their lives had changed for the better. The survivors said they had deeper spiritual awareness and greater inner strength. They were mindful of how they spent their time, e.g., with friends and family. They felt life overall had more meaning, and they were reevaluating their lives toward better outcomes.

My experience mirrored what these two researchers heard from people they interviewed, many of whom had experienced traumatic events such as death, diseases like cancer, or life-changing accidents. However, the suffering that resulted from these horrifying experiences was not an endpoint but rather the beginning. Instead, it acted as a catalyst, pushing these people toward positive change.

Since Tedeschi and Calhoun's findings, researchers worldwide have begun delving into posttraumatic growth. Studies have found more than half of trauma survivors report positive change. These included new possibilities relating to others, personal strength, spiritual transformation, and appreciation of life, far more than the much better-known posttraumatic stress disorder report (Kleber, 2019). This emerging field of psychological research shows how the suffering caused by traumatic events can be harnessed as a force for self-improvement and success rather than destruction.

Geology professor Sally Walker was among the survivors of a plane bound for Los Angeles that crashed during takeoff in Taiwan. According to *CNN*, eighty-three of the 179 people aboard Singapore Airlines Flight 006 were killed in the crash. The 747 jetliner reportedly hit an object on the runway during a storm and sent flaming wreckage flying across the tarmac at Taipei's Chiang Kai-shek International Airport at 11:48 p.m. There were conflicting reports of what the jet hit. *CNN* reported some witnesses said a wind shear slammed the plane to the ground, where it then exploded into flames. Sally Walker called the geology department to let her colleagues know of the crash and that she was safe. She suffered a deep gash on her leg and was hospitalized. But, she said, "When I got home, the sky was brighter, I paid attention to the texture of the sidewalks. It was like being in a movie. ... Now everything is a gift" (Rubner, 2000). Surviving that airline crash opened up an entire part of her awareness that she would never have known about otherwise.

Posttraumatic growth can be transformative and powerful, but it does not always start there. For some of us, traumatic events are followed by posttraumatic stress disorder before we can access posttraumatic growth. This means we endure the daily struggles, the emotional and physical pain associated with trauma, and then years later we understand how the traumatic event informed our lives and how, because of the suffering, our lives were unquestionably better.

There are many inspirational stories, and I am proud to say each is exceptional. However, one narrative in particular stood out for me, which can be found in episode eight of *Surviving Trauma: Stories of Hope*. Rosalind was born to parents who would be sent to prison for sexual crimes when she was only five years old, and both her parents became registered as sex offenders. Rosalind and her sisters were sent to foster care, where they survived for a few years before being adopted by a great aunt. Life presented little Rosalind with neglect, malnutrition, and abuse challenges, among others, during that time. At the age of twelve, she was confronted and told she would have to leave home when she turned eighteen. This thought caused much anxiety and sleepless nights for a little girl who was now wondering how to make money to pay rent for a place to live and pay for electricity when she turned eighteen.

Despite everything that had happened to her, the feeling of being alone caused the most damage. Even though she had her two sisters with her, they knew they would not be able to take care of each other. Yet, despite this being a lonely and grim experience, there was hope that this experience would end. Knowing it would not last forever brought with it freedom and reassurance that she would eventually leave and create her own life. What we learn here from her story is everything has a beginning, middle, and end.

With the possibility of an end, she knew she would owe her abusers no obligation because they showed no obligation to her. This thought, coupled with a deep inner knowing that there was something bigger watching over her, gave her the determination to survive the years that followed. After turning eighteen in November, she was met with a duffel bag at the door in the heart of the January winter and told to leave. The social grant had stopped, leaving no need for her to continue staying with her adoptive parents.

She left and, having the foresight and being resourceful, joined the military, specifically the United States Air Force, where she stayed for several years and built a solid career in information technology. She was deployed to different locations throughout her career, and she was exposed to another side of life and gained alternative life experiences. Finally, at the age of thirty, she decided to change careers. She went back to school, earned a BA in psychology, obtained a master's in social work, and became a therapist.

When I asked her what tools she used during her trauma recovery, she shared that military life offered regular and ongoing therapy. She also continued treatment after the military and focused on recognizing the wounded and unnurtured child. She learned to love and nurture her inner child, reassuring her what happened was not okay. She shared with me her inner child should not have had to be that strong, but she was proud of the little girl for getting her to where she is today. Her message of hope is she should not have had to be so strong, and these terrible things should not have happened to her, but she is happy that little Rosalind had the strength to hang on for dear life and get through it. Her story reminds us that even on the worst of days, we can survive.

Spirituality and religion also played a role in her trauma recovery. She shared on my podcast that initially, she was not sure God's plan was good, and she recommended in a tongue-in-cheek way that God get himself a planner. Through a solid foundation of religion and spirituality, she can understand how her experiences inform her work and practice. Today she can assist others because she knows firsthand what trauma looks and feels like. She can now see God's bigger picture. She is anchored in her faith and confirms she always knew there was something out there looking out for her and watching over her. Today, through her work, she provides services to foster kids who are emancipating from the system and provides trauma-informed therapy services.

When I heard Rosalind's impactful and inspirational story, I had to pause and think. The lesson I took from her story was that as much as our experiences happen to us, they happen for us. In life, we tend to experience our challenges as anchors, but every day we have the opportunity to choose whether we want to be a victim of our circumstances or a survivor. What inspired me and what I found to be empowering about her story was she allowed her traumatic experiences to inform her work and who she is today.

However, growth is not an automatic handout following trauma. Instead, the road of progression begins with healing from trauma, and it does not come without suffering. However, we know people can do far more than heal, based on the science produced by researchers. Given the right environment and mindset, survivors of traumatic experiences can change, using the trauma, the suffering, and daily struggle that ensues as an opportunity to reflect, reevaluate, search for meaning and purpose in their lives, and ultimately become better versions of themselves. The same holds for me, because from this point in my life, I understand how the posttrauma experience opened a path that helped me heal and grow to step out of trauma into joy and find inner peace.

CHAPTER TWO:

TALK ABOUT IT

—

"Just because no one else can heal or do your inner work for you doesn't mean you can, should, or need to do it alone."
—LISA OLIVERA

While Captain van der Merwe led the manhunt, the paramedics rushed to take me to the hospital for medical attention. The paramedics wheeled me into a room where I was met by a female doctor, who was the district surgeon at the local government hospital. She was responsible for the processing of my body and collecting evidence. She was compassionate yet matter of fact. She asked detailed questions about the rape such as, "Was the penetration oral, vaginal, anal, or all of the above?" These questions forced me to relive the events of that day, and as difficult and horrifying as it was, I knew cooperating would aid the overall investigation, so I answered all her questions, essentially talking about what happened for the second time. I watched as she collected evidence and bagged my underwear and clothes. I recognized the voice of the police captain coming from outside the examination room. The captain had good news for my family and me: Three arrests had been made. Later, I was discharged with antiretroviral medication as a precautionary measure in case I had been infected with HIV. My small trauma was within my big trauma. The next day I was admitted to a private hospital where I was assigned a team of doctors who helped with the physical healing. The team included a primary physician; ophthalmologists; an ear, nose, and throat specialist; a neurologist; a gynecologist; a psychologist and an orthopedic surgeon.

Following my discharge from the private hospital two weeks later, I attended my very first outpatient therapy session. My parents drove me to the appointment, and, as always, we were on time. It was a hot day, and I remember the practice being a refreshing air-conditioned place. We waited in the waiting room while my dad completed the administration documents. Finally, a brown door to the right of the reception area opened, and a tall man appeared and invited us in. The psychologist was a slender man with light-framed glasses, kind eyes, and a welcoming demeanor. I first met him in my hospital room during my private hospital stay following the brutal attack at the apartment.

In the office, there was a wall-to-wall bookshelf behind a dark wooded desk. To the one side of the room, there was a couch with an armchair positioned opposite of the sofa. A small table with a glass of water, clipboard, and pen was next to the armchair. The psychologist walked ahead of us and signaled for us to take a seat. He took a seat in the armchair, crossed his legs, and picked up the clipboard and pen.

After the initial introductions, the psychologist gathered some information about us. My parents explained the events at the apartment that led up to our visit. My parents were excused, and after they left the room to wait in the waiting area, the focus was on me. It was my turn to speak, but I could not find the words. I kept thinking this was my story, and it was a very personal one, one I did not necessarily want to share. It was not because I felt judged or that the questions asked were out of curiosity, but something inside kept me from sharing freely. I answered most of the questions, however, but with great difficulty. I realized I did not want to go to the place in my head that held the information, because every time I thought about it, I was not recalling a memory; instead, I was reliving the horrifying experience, and it was awful. After our session concluded, I was asked to leave the room while my parents reentered. I waited in the cool waiting area. The next time the door to the right of the reception area opened, my parents appeared with the psychologist. They shook hands, and we left with an appointment card indicating the next session and a prescription for medication.

This was all so foreign to us. Until that point, no one in my family had seen a psychologist or had prescribed medication for mental health issues. I was the first in our family to be diagnosed with posttraumatic stress disorder. I was also informed I had a chemical imbalance in my brain and suffered from anxiety. As a treatment, I received psychotherapy and medication. The circumstances that led to this point were so overwhelming that there was not much time to process. We accepted this was what happened following a traumatic experience, and we were content to comply.

At this point, let's explore what therapy is. According to the American Psychological Association, in psychotherapy, also called talk therapy or usually just "therapy," psychologists help people of all ages live happier, healthier, and more productive lives. Psychologists apply research-based techniques to help people develop more effective habits. Several approaches to psychotherapy, including cognitive-behavioral, interpersonal, and psychodynamic, among others, help people work through their problems. Psychotherapy is a collaborative treatment based on the relationship between an individual and a psychologist. A psychologist provides a supportive environment that allows you to talk openly in an objective, neutral, and nonjudgmental space. Most therapy focuses on individuals, although psychotherapists also work with couples, families, and groups.

Both the patient and therapist need to be actively involved in psychotherapy. The trust and relationship between a person and their therapist is essential to working together effectively and benefiting from psychotherapy. Psychotherapy can be short term (a few sessions) for immediate issues or long term (months or years), dealing with longstanding and complex problems. The treatment goals and arrangements for how often and how long to meet are planned jointly by the patient and therapist.

Confidentiality is an essential requirement of psychotherapy. Also, although patients share personal feelings and thoughts, intimate physical contact with a therapist is never appropriate, acceptable, or valuable. Psychotherapy is often used in combination with medication to treat mental health conditions. In some circumstances, medication may be helpful, and psychotherapy may be the best option in others. However, for many people, combined medication and psychotherapy treatment is better than either alone. In addition, healthy lifestyle improvements, such as good nutrition, regular exercise, and adequate sleep, can be crucial in supporting recovery and overall wellness.

So, does psychotherapy work? Research shows most people who receive psychotherapy experience symptom relief and are better able to function in their lives. About 75 percent of people who enter psychotherapy offer some benefit from it (American Psychiatric Association, 2019). Psychotherapy has been shown to improve emotions and behaviors and can be linked with positive changes in the brain and body. The benefits include fewer sick days, less disability, fewer medical problems, and increased work satisfaction.

With brain imaging techniques, researchers have been able to see changes in the brain after a person has undergone psychotherapy. Numerous studies have identified brain changes in people with mental illness (including depression, panic disorder, posttraumatic stress disorder, and other conditions) because of undergoing psychotherapy. However, in most cases, the brain changes resulting from psychotherapy were similar to changes resulting from medication (Karlsson, 2011).

To help get the most out of psychotherapy, approach therapy as a collaborative effort, be open and honest, and follow your agreed-upon treatment plan. Follow through with any assignments between sessions, such as journal writing or practicing what you've talked about.

Several years after my first therapy visit, my older sister and I were looking forward to a visit from our mom. Usually, my parents visited together, but this time it was only my mom. We helped Mom unpack and settle in for her stay. She was going through an emotionally challenging time, and it showed. I watched with great sadness as she struggled with the emotions as they all boiled to the surface. The truth is my mom had been carrying a heavy burden that included life, health, job, finances, and marital strain.

The challenges caused an increase in anxiety and worry, affecting her social relationships, her trust in other people, her security, and her sense of belonging. I wanted to help my mom; after all, she has been there for me all my life. I did not want her to suffer and carry the burdens by herself.

Given my personal experience in trauma recovery and therapy, I knew she could benefit from therapy and talking to someone about the issues weighing her down. Therapy added value to my life, and I knew it could do the same for my mom. I wanted to be the ray of light for her.

After lunch, we retired to the lounge area at home. I then took the opportunity and suggested that she meet with a psychologist. To my surprise, the suggestion was met with resistance as she cited the barriers to therapy, the first being, "Therapy is not for me; it's for crazy people. I can deal with my problems on my own." As I listened in shock, I remembered that therapy was not the solution in my mom's culture or generation. They did not consider it an option. Instead, the belief was you had to deal with your problems privately. Therapy also carried a lot of stigmas, and the potential judgment from others was a major barrier to seeking help. The idea people may think that something happened to you, that something is wrong with you, or that you are crazy was enough.

In a *Psychology Today* article, Dr. Dana Gionta explained that while at the bank, she was asked by the bank teller, "What kind of doctor are you?" "I'm a psychologist," she said. "A clinical psychologist?" the teller asked. She replied, "Yes…" Then he said, "You must deal with a lot of crazy people." She was both amused and somewhat surprised. She then paused and carefully thought about how she was going to answer this, without adding to his already unfortunate stereotypical view of the profession. She replied, "Well, actually, I work most often with people dealing with difficult life transitions, like divorce, health challenges, relocation, work stress, and family/parenting issues." "So, where is your practice located?" he asked. At this point, the teller lowered his voice and half-whispered something to her, but she could not make out what he said, although she thought he was trying to establish how much she had charged. The other bank teller started to look curiously at him and their exchange. As the banking transaction was nearing an end, he finally asked, "Do you have a business card?" She gave him her card, thanked him for his help, and walked away, wondering where and when her next encounter of "stigma" would be.

Unfortunately, to this day, the realm of therapy or counseling remains quite mysterious to most people. Let's be honest: not everybody wants to rush out to see a psychologist, therapist, or psychiatrist. It's not the type of thing in which someone wakes up in the morning and says, "Wow, I've been missing something in my life. I'd love to chat to a stranger about my innermost personal fears, thoughts, and feelings and see exactly how messed up I am."

Most people think just the opposite about almost any health or mental health appointment. They avoid them like the plague, and it is not something they want to deal with. There are many questions and barriers to accessing mental health services, like what happens in that room. They might ask themselves, "If I go to a therapist, does that mean I'm crazy, weak, or a failure? What will others think? What if I'm seen coming out of that kind of office?"

According to a March 2017 *Clinical Review* article, research has shown many trauma survivors seem to be reluctant to seek professional help. A systematic research review to classify the barriers and facilitators regarding mental health service utilization in a *Science Direct* article identified nineteen studies addressing military personnel and seventeen studies with trauma survivors of the general population. The data analysis revealed the most prominent barriers included concerns related to stigma, shame and rejection, low mental health literacy, lack of knowledge and treatment-related doubts, fear of negative social consequences, limited resources, time, and expenses. Another prominent finding, according to *Science Direct*, was trauma survivors face specific trauma-related barriers to mental health service use, especially with concerns about reexperiencing the traumatic events. Many trauma survivors avoid reminders and are therefore concerned about dealing with certain memories in treatment. These are valid concerns, but unfortunately many people like my mom decided not to seek help despite experiencing significant emotional, physical, or mental distress.

The truth is most people who attend therapy sessions are there to deal with everyday life struggles, not a serious mental illness. In our lives, we are constantly challenged by chronic work-related stressors, career issues, financial problems, health issues or a recent health diagnosis, family or parent/child conflict, cultural assimilation, and academic issues. People also deal with difficult life cycle-related transitions, like the death of a family member or friend, the ending of a romantic relationship or close friendship, family/couple changes related to the addition of a child, getting married or divorced, caregiving for sick or disabled loved ones, and decision-making challenges related to these life choices.

In my first psychology session, I experienced internal resistance leading to hesitancy about the idea of talking about the trauma with a psychologist. Yet, as time passed, I realized that in therapy, I did not have to relive my traumatic experiences in every session or even talk about them. It was not necessarily the event that took precedence in the discussion, but it was how it affected my life afterward that became the points of discussion. It impacted me on an everyday basis, my relationships with friends and family, my health, my academic performance, my romantic relationships, and so on. I realized the traumatic event happened and I could not change that, but I could engage with issues that arose as a result of the way my life was impacted following trauma. This realization was a huge breakthrough for me.

My view slowly started to change from the initial resistance that I felt at the first appointment to a more holistic approach to healing my mental health. l came to realize talk therapy is an effective tool that can help beyond trauma, and I did not have to do the healing work alone or only be confined to the traumatic experience. I understood psychologists and therapists are trained professionals and I was in good hands. At the point when I was experiencing internal resistance, it was possible to think solving my problems on my own meant that I was strong; however, I realized strength lies in being vulnerable. In deliberately seeking help, even when that was difficult, I was doing something much braver than just ignoring those problems and letting them get worse.

In a recent interview, I spoke to therapist Rosalind Pistilli, who helped me identify barriers and bust the myths about therapy. She shared with me there is a general belief that if someone goes to treatment, they admit something happened to them. Unfortunately, the word "trauma therapy" can sometimes transport a potential client to the past, which can be very scary. Hence, she tells her clients, "Trauma therapy is simple, but it's not easy." It's simple enough to create an inviting space together, but making the first appointment is not easy. The hardest part of therapy is making the appointment and being willing to walk through the door.

While walking through the door can be challenging, it can also be intimidating to talk to a stranger about painful life experiences. Rosalind says it's a little different from talking to somebody like your mom because the person sharing is processing their feelings around a loved one, which serves a similar purpose but is, at the same time, different. In this regard, I was fortunate to speak to Anissa Tolliver, who is also a licensed therapist. In our discussion, she helped me understand that, despite the barriers mentioned in this chapter, some people may have barriers imposed by their culture. She shared the story that as an African American woman, she grew up in a household where the rule was, "What happens in this house stays in this house." That meant that if something happened or was bothering you, you were not allowed to speak about it outside the home. In her circumstances, she had to find alternative ways to access talk therapy closer to home. For her, she found that with her grandfather. He was the trusted confidant that provided the ear to listen, the shoulder to cry on, guidance, and most importantly, a safe space to share.

According to Rosalind, the word "trauma" holds a lot of weight in the decision to seek therapy. She believes part of destigmatizing therapy is destigmatizing our trauma rights if we recognize that nearly everybody has had painful experiences. So, when we frame the discussion around experiences instead of using the vernacular "trauma," people tend to feel they are simply casually talking about things that bother them rather than talking about deep traumatic experiences. Using the pandemic as an example to illustrate the concept of reframing trauma, Rosalind explained we are all collectively being traumatized by this worldwide pandemic. If we now talk about trauma therapy for everyone, that distracts from the work we're doing when a word brings up immediate mental images of what we are all going through; so one of the ways to not do that is by not saying that word "trauma," making it a little less intimidating and a little more approachable.

But when we think of trauma therapy, people feel they have to relive their experiences, which can be extremely painful and sometimes embarrassing. There could also potentially be a lot of shame associated with the trauma, for example, somebody from the military who may have participated in acts of war they're not proud of. This creates resistance to trauma therapy, and the forms of resistance from clients include not wanting to rehash past experiences, not showing emotion by crying, and showing their vulnerabilities. The other side of the coin is that very rarely is trauma the person's fault. In Rosalind's case, her childhood traumas were inflicted upon her, and she was not an active participant in her trauma.

Another form of resistance exists in the person questioning why they have to undergo therapy if the perpetrator was the one who committed the offense. In this form of resistance, they do not see themselves as victims, and at this crucial point, Rosalind reminds her clients of the important fact they are the survivors.

Denial is another form of resistance. As the science of trauma tells us, our brain protects us from emotional pain, and we bury the emotional wounds from our trauma in a deep place within ourselves. The challenge with denial is if left untreated, the emotions will boil to the surface at the most inconvenient time.

Finding a new therapist is another form of resistance. Having been on both sides of the couch, Rosalind did not enjoy making this change in her therapy journey. However, she changes therapists smoothly because there is a massive misconception that you have to rehash the past when you see a new therapist. The reality is it is not always necessary to start at the beginning or relive the traumatic event. The starting point is about what bothers you and impacts your current state of functioning. If, during that session, you organically connect to a traumatic event or your childhood, then that event can be addressed. You make the connection independently without the therapist telling you, and that is a powerful moment that can propel progress because it happened organically.

Impatience is another form of resistance. Clients will say, "I have a lot of trauma, and I want to get it out because I want to get on with my life." If this client lives in a toxic environment and attends a one-hour session without receiving radiation from the toxic home environment, working on the trauma is like slapping Band-Aids on a gaping wound. From a therapist's perspective, she recommends that you must be in a safe, supportive environment to work on the trauma. Once you start the trauma work, the therapist addresses what is bothering you in the present and touches gently on past traumatic, painful experiences that may be blocking forward progression.

Digging deep is not recommended if you are in a toxic environment. Rosalind gives her clients clear instructions to keep hydrated, get rest, and give themselves time to have a couple of days of not wanting to get out of bed because the brain is healing. To ultimately heal the wound, it has to be through both mental and physical work. In general, people go to therapy to feel better, but sometimes it will worsen before it gets better, and it's not a linear progression. So not every therapy session is smooth sailing, but she says we have room for growth when we get to that point.

So, I asked, if this is the case, why is it important to receive trauma therapy? Trauma therapy is about accountability; it's about identifying what belongs to the other person and what belongs to us. For example, self-blame is sometimes associated with car accident survivors. A car accident has a solid start and finishing time as something that we know as a resolvable trauma. During therapy, survivors will say, "I should never have gotten behind the wheel." Rosalind can't argue that logic, because if you remove yourself from the equation, the equation does not exist. Why shouldn't you have been on that highway? How much responsibility do you have for the fact that this other person was driving intoxicated or was texting while driving? In this scenario, it helps to identify what we are responsible for. So, it is crucial to identify and release emotions such as shame and guilt from such a traumatic event if it does not belong to you.

Trauma therapy is also helpful to restore joy, activities, and safety in our lives. To demonstrate this, Rosalind shared a personal story about being bullied in middle school and high school, preventing her from initially going to college. In therapy, she addressed the fact that bullying kept her from pursuing a college degree without regurgitating the painful experience of being bullied. At the same time, if a survivor of childhood trauma says, "My parents abused me as a child, and as a result, I have decided not to have children because I am afraid that I will do the same," you can process all of that without going into detail about the abuse, what they did, how often it happened, and so forth. During therapy, the limiting belief of not having children out of fear from the trauma will be addressed. How responsible is a five-year-old for their parent's abuse? We will not place accountability on a five-year-old. It is about providing reassurance that the ownership of emotions taken on as adults does not belong to them.

Trauma therapy tries to recognize what link exists between what happened in the past and what is happening in the present. Many traumatic experiences don't impact our present and future, and we do not need them to be resolved. However, it becomes relevant when it affects the present. For example, growing up, there was a tree in Rosalind's family's garden in which there was a bird's nest. Her mother warned Rosalind and her friends not to approach or play with the nest. As we find with kids, Rosalind and her friends did not listen to her mom about leaving the robin's nest in the tree alone. Instead, they tipped the branch over, and all the eggs flew out of the nest and got smashed on the ground. Witnessing the consequences of their actions left Rosalind to reflect on their actions. As she realized with horror what had happened, Rosalind recalls crying for hours because she realized "they had killed the babies." This is an apparent traumatic experience from her childhood. However, it does not prevent her from making progress. If Rosalind were still overwhelmed by guilt whenever she saw baby birds, then trauma therapy could help her move on.

Overall, when it comes to therapy, the bad news is you have trauma, and the best part is it can be treated and recovery is 100 percent possible. Trauma cannot heal until it is heard. The barriers and resistance we encounter can be addressed, and therapy is a safe space to do so. You will not be made to feel stigma or shame or have to relive the traumatic event. Talk therapy can be formalized in the form of therapy, or it can also be informal, like discussions with friends or family members.

In conclusion, there is no reason to fear talking about our traumatic experiences that limit our lives. However, there is no easy way to get over our fear, anxiety, and reservations that prevent us from seeking a safe space to heal. Having these feelings about talking—in or out of therapy—is a normal part of our lives and lets us know we're about to embark on a scary journey of self-discovery. What is important is that we talk about our limitations, whether with a therapist in trauma therapy or with a friend, family member, or religious leader. In this process, we will learn things about ourselves along the way and find opportunities to bring happiness, a joy to activities, and safety into our lives.

So instead of fighting or suppressing negative feelings, it's best to accept them as a part of the process. That acceptance becomes one of the first steps of getting help in the psychotherapeutic process of change. Without making changes and taking accountability in our life, we will continue to suffer.

CHAPTER THREE:

THE STRUGGLE TO DECIDE

"May your choices reflect your hopes, not your fears."
—NELSON MANDELA

Following the murder attempt on my life, I found myself left with this deep desire to give back. During that time, I often thought about the police captain with the beautiful blue eyes who stared down at me in my hour of need, ready to serve and rescue. I wanted to be the "blue eyes" for someone else, meaning I wanted to give hope and assurance of safety to someone in need like the captain did for me. I knew I wanted to give back, but becoming a police officer seemed like a daunting task that could take a long time, and I needed something more attainable and immediate, like being a volunteer. One day, I got the bright idea to contact the team of paramedics that helped me on the scene of the crime to enquire about volunteer work. I was in luck, and there was an opening to work with the team as a volunteer, and I took it.

When I started volunteering, I was assigned to a paramedic team that operated from a day hospital in a crime-ridden area. Volunteering was an exciting experience because the need for help was so vast. We dealt with different calls from domestic violence incidents, dehydrated babies, stabbings, motor vehicle accidents, strokes, and heart attacks. When we were not out on the road on a dispatch call, we helped in the emergency room. One particular Friday night, a group of young men ran into the ER. They had been involved in a gang fight and sought refuge in the ER as a place of safety and medical treatment.

The ER doctor asked me to assist him while he examined the patient, one of the men who ran into the hospital. The man was covering the side of his face with his T-shirt. The doctor assessed the wound to establish where the bleeding originated. He asked me to hold the light for him to see inside the mouth, and as I assisted, I saw the doctors' fingers protrude from the side of the man's cheek. He had been stabbed in the face, slicing through the cheek and the tongue. He was eighteen years old and crying like a baby.

There was no tough gangster in the ER, just a kid out of his depth. We worked our way through all the patients, and the last one from the group we examined was nine years old. I showed him to the examination room and made light conversation. This boy was part of the same gang as the others. He, too, had been in the knife fight late that Friday night. Despite the brave face he tried to put up, I could tell he was a scared child.

The following day when the shift ended, I found myself questioning my choice to be a volunteer following everything I experienced that Friday night. I set out to be the "blue eyes" for victims and people in general who needed medical attention following trauma. Despite the many positive dispatch calls where I could help someone in need, I was faced with assisting perpetrators too that night. As a volunteer, I showed empathy and compassion toward the patients, but that night I changed. I wanted to reserve my empathy, compassion, hope, and understanding for someone I deemed deserving. Instead of continuing to rescue the world through volunteer work, I quit and brought my need to help into my relationships, which became my pattern of addiction.

In all my relationships, whether family, romantic, or even at work, I took on this self-assigned role and helped others at my expense. In my family relationships, I would help and support more than required. In my work relationships, I would take on responsibilities that were not mine. I nurtured partners with unprocessed trauma and addictions such as alcohol, drugs, spending, thought, and intellect in my romantic relationships. When it came to thought and intellect as an addiction, my partner would think about his emotions rather than feel them. He used thought and intellect to suppress emotions and would thrive on processing someone else's emotions.

With hindsight and a lot of healing work, I can quickly identify this pattern of behavior now, but at the time I was oblivious.

This need to help landed me in several codependent relationships. According to a *PsychCentral* article written by Crystal Raypole and reviewed by Vara Saripalli, PsyD, codependency is a way of behaving in relationships. Experts originally introduced the term "codependency" in the 1940s to help describe specific behavior patterns they noticed in partners and family members of people living with alcohol use disorder. By this original definition, "codependent" might describe loved ones who "enabled" alcohol use by making excuses, hiding the alcohol use, and protecting the person from any fallout or consequences of their actions.

However, according to the *PsychCentral* article, experts today agree codependency has a more nuanced and complex meaning—and can show up in many situations, not just ones involving substance use. Codependency refers to any enmeshed relationship in which one person loses their sense of independence and believes they need to tend to someone else.

According to a 2018 research review, "The lived experience of codependency: an Interpretative Phenomenological Analysis," codependent behavior patterns generally involve four main themes: self-sacrifice; a tendency to focus on others; a need for control, which may fuel conflict; and difficulty recognizing and expressing emotions.

These themes can show up across various types of relationships—and even how you relate to yourself.

My partner and I started like any other couple. We met and fell in love and planned to spend our lives together. We decided to move in and build a home. Shortly after moving in together, my partner would spoil me by running a bath at the end of a long day and having a romantic home-cooked dinner together. I was showered with gifts, luxury holidays, financial comfort, and a plush lifestyle. Despite being fiercely independent and earning my keep, I enjoyed our relationship and the attention.

Soon the emotional abuse started leaving me feeling helpless. It was subtle at first, but it became more blatant over time. It started with his highlighting all that I could not do. He would say things like, "You can't cook," "You expect me to eat this? I don't want this," or "You can't grocery shop, all you buy is crap," or he would make comments such as "typical." Over time I started to change my behavior to accommodate the view by giving the grocery money to him, allowing him to cook, and not participating in those activities because I started believing I was not good at it.

The romantic baths and dinners quickly became a way to ensure I was home at a specific time from work or any social activity. I was not allowed to watch particular channels on TV. It was not as if he said, "You don't watch that channel," but if I watched a channel he disapproved of, his mood immediately changed and became very tense. The activity of watching the show would be picked apart until I started to question why I was watching anyway and changing the channel was an easy option to escape the tension that was building in the room. Instead of addressing this issue, I started avoiding those channels and mostly watched what he wanted to keep the peace. When I got dressed, he would make comments like, "Are you leaving the house like that?"

leaving me to feel like something was wrong with the way I dressed, so I changed my clothes and eventually my style.

The control became worse when my friends and family were mistreated. When they came to visit, they would be disrespected, put down, and humiliated. I remember my sister visiting and me offering her a seat to join us for dinner. My partner was asleep after binge-drinking on the couch, and when he woke up, he asked my sister in front of everyone at the table, "Who told you to come to my house and eat my food? Did I invite you here?" The humiliation and shame were overwhelming for me. As usual, I could not see his faults, and eventually very few people came around, leaving me isolated, feeling trapped like I had no other choice but to stay in that situation and not leave him. On the rare occasion that I left the house to meet a friend, he would constantly call until it was so embarrassing that leaving and going home was more manageable.

Any idea that I had to do something new, for example, writing a book, would be criticized and put down. I was told, "All you have are pipe dreams," or, "Do you think you can?" I slowly started believing this narrative. Over time, these mean-spirited comments began to break down my self-worth, making the idea of a better life outside the relationship impossible.

I would walk on eggshells trying to navigate any situation that could set him off. It was highly anxiety provoking and stressful living only to keep another person happy and content at my expense. I could feel how I was losing who I was, the essence of me, my sense of self day by day, month by month, year by year. However, my intuition was strong, and it alerted me to the fact my life had a purpose. Listening to my intuition helped me to decide to leave, but even after I made the decision and had a plan, there was no action because I was plagued with doubt. The years of mental abuse had taken their toll.

To access the mindset that allowed me to tap into my courage, I had to release all the responsibilities of helping others at my expense. I started with the easier things in life, like saying no to friends and family for something I had taken on that they could carry themselves. It was challenging to do but liberating because it allowed me to set healthy boundaries and execute the decision to leave.

The circumstances surrounding abuse look different for everyone, and as much as I was going through one version of it, my friend Robyn Russell was experiencing the other. She met her abuser during a year working abroad in the United States. She remembered the thrill of living abroad, the excitement of starting her own life away from South Africa, her family, her church, and the mission work she had been involved with her whole life. After a year abroad, Robyn and her abuser continued a long-distance relationship. At first, the relationship seemed beautiful, with gentle, kind gestures that would steal her heart, such as the effort made with writing and mailing letters, incurring the expense of international phone cards to hear each other's voices.

Robyn's parents had always been involved in mission work. They fostered several medically fragile and terminally ill children throughout her upbringing, and she was involved in the care of these children. Unfortunately, after returning to South Africa from her year abroad in the United States, her parents had to leave the country, leaving her to care for yet another terminally ill baby who sadly passed away in her arms. Watching the baby pass away was a traumatic experience that left Robyn emotionally drained and questioning her life choices. At that time, her abuser made the trip to visit her in South Africa. He proposed, and Robyn accepted despite unacceptable behavior patterns during his visit.

Robyn was a tomboy growing up and had many male friends, and during the visit, she introduced her friends to her abuser. She explained there had been warning signs she overlooked at that stage, such as sudden fits of anger and rage, which included emotional abuse and name-calling. She explained her abuser felt so threatened after meeting some of her male friends that he slammed the car door so hard that the passenger window shattered after returning home. Despite these concerns from friends about his behavior and intentions, Robyn was getting married. This was her escape to a world abroad that she lived in and loved for a year and could have again. Little did she know her dream was about to become a fourteen-year nightmare.

Robyn was raised in a loving home with two parents who are best friends. They never displayed any signs of abuse or violence, they rarely argued, and they would immediately apologize or attempt to reach common ground if they disagreed. This relationship between her parents led Robyn to believe that a marriage was not hard work; in fact, being friends made the union of marriage exciting, free, and peaceful for her parents. Following her wedding, the happy couple departed for their honeymoon, a period of harmony and celebration of the union and their future together. During their stay at the resort, they got into an argument the first night at dinner. Robyn was accused of being too friendly with the waiter during dinner service.

Little did she know that basic courtesy like thanking a waiter with a smile had severe consequences. After returning to the room, her abuser struck her for the first time. She was punched on her honeymoon.

She describes that she was filled with shame, fear, embarrassment, and humiliation in those moments. Confiding in her parents and closest friends did not seem possible. Later the couple returned from their honeymoon and left South Africa to start their life together, where they would, over time, raise three daughters.

As soon as they arrived in the United States, the abuse became more frequent and violent. It initially started with punches to the skull because the swelling and the bruising were not visible under her thick head of hair. Shortly after, he punched her and broke her nose, so she quit her job because she could not face her colleagues with the bruising. The incidents of physical abuse continued time and again. One time, he headbutted her in the middle of her forehead, which split her eyebrow and resulted in a trip to the ER. The amount of blood was surprising, and the laceration required eight stitches. When asked the standard question about domestic abuse, Robyn remembered the words of her abuser: "If you call the cops or report what happened, by the time they showed up, you would be dead." In her mind, she was screaming, "Yes, he did this to me, please help me," but instead chose to cover up the abuse. She told how she tripped up the deck steps and busted her head while carrying groceries.

The abuse was not only physical but emotional and financial. Robyn says she chose to work because he allowed her to. Upon her first arrival in the United States, she worked in minimal income jobs, and he decided what to do with her income. It was used to pay for day care, and she would be granted money for gas to get to work. On the rare occasion they could go to a restaurant, she was given a budget for her food and drink, and should she go over budget, she had to reimburse the difference to her abuser.

The abuse would also extend to the children. Still, when the abuser directed his anger at the kids, Robyn would protect her daughters from beatings by interjecting and deflecting so he would redirect his rage on her. Despite these attempts to save and shelter them from the abuse, she could not shelter them from everything. They heard the screaming and yelling behind closed doors, the slapping or shoving into the wall or on the ground. Her eldest daughter vividly recalls an incident in which Robyn's abuser broke a dustpan over her head. Robyn had forgotten the incident because it was one of the less abusive attacks.

For the longest time, pride, shame, and embarrassment kept her shackled. Her inner dialogue was debating suffering in silence versus reporting her abuser. She felt confiding in her parents or close friends back home in South Africa would leave them feeling helpless and worried, so she never did. Instead, she told herself she decided to marry him to move to another county, so it was only fitting that the consequences were hers to carry. She worried about where she would end up with her daughters should she leave this abusive situation. She could foresee losing her home and becoming homeless. She feared her abuser's family would accuse her of being a bad mother and take her kids. In her mind, there was nobody who could take her in in the middle of the night with three kids and a suitcase.

Her abuser didn't allow her to have friends. The ones she made had to be kept at a distance and in the dark about the abuse. She tried to confide in friends who would ignore her cry for help and continue the conversation like it never happened, but one friend heard her cry for help and offered to be there if she ever decided to leave. With no family or close support in the United States, all options seemed like the worst outcome, so she stayed because she could not see that leaving could result in a better life for her and her daughters.

Slowly, her inner dialogue started to change. She decided to empower herself through education and finances. She applied for a student loan and started college without her abuser's support. He would use most of the student loan to pay for day care for the kids, but she managed to make the payments to the college despite this attempt to sabotage her.

Over the years that followed, she stayed focused despite the abuse. She quickly worked her way up the ladder to a job working from home that allowed her to be close to her daughters. During that time, she saved to afford anticipated legal fees for a divorce, a roof over their heads, and a better quality of life for her girls.

Finally, Robyn had a plan and the means, but executing and leaving the abusive situation was more difficult than anticipated. She found herself knowing what to do but not making the decision and taking action despite being in a position to do so. While she was paralyzed to make the decision, the abuse continued. The pivotal moment was after a farewell dinner for friends.

She told me her abuser had too much to drink at the restaurant and started acting belligerent. The embarrassment she felt was overwhelming, but she pushed through. He grabbed the steering wheel from her on the drive home, and she fought back while the vehicle swerved across the road. After gaining control of the car and pulling into the driveway of their home, he grabbed her arm and bit her as hard as he could while holding her down.

She describes she felt as if a pit bull was attacking her. Her saving grace was a passing neighbor walking his dog. He saw them pull in and knocked on the passenger window to say hello. When they heard the knock, he released the teeth grip, and she made her escape into the house, where she locked and barricaded the bedroom door to protect her and the kids. She describes the bruising from her shoulder to her elbow as a tattoo sleeve. That night, something in her changed. Despite the abuse she loved him, but at that stage all hope, respect, love, feelings of affection, and loyalty, as warped as it was, were gone. There was nothing left, no more pieces of her to give.

Knowing what she knew then, Robyn went back to her plan but still did not decide and execute.

Months went by, and one day, her abuser took a tool from the garage and destroyed their home. He smashed mirrors, walls, and doors while shouting, "This is where you call home. You have no family here. Nowhere else to go. So now, this can be your beautiful 'home.'" She and her daughters were terrified, but she found the strength to file a police report and a restraining order. Finally, she took the step of making a decision and following through. When she finally sat the kids down to inform them that she was also filing for a divorce, her oldest daughter's response was, "It's about time."

Up until then, Robyn thought she was protecting her girls through self-sacrifice for their benefit, but she realized in retrospect the decision to stay harmed her kids in many ways. As a result, her girls grew up with a very skewed view about love, relationships, men, and marriage. In hindsight, she regretted staying as long as she did and exposing her children to a toxic, abusive environment for fourteen years. After filing the police report and the restraining order, Robyn called her friend who had offered years before to be there when the day finally came, and she was ready to help by booking a hotel for Robyn and the three girls to stay. The years that followed were challenging, but they were no longer in a toxic environment.

Continuing with her self-improvement and embarking on her healing journey, Robyn enrolled herself in a program called Divorce Care, which was run by a local pastor. The program provided a guide book that allowed for reflection and provided biblical guidance for healing and forgiveness. During the healing journey, she learned to accept love freely, give love freely, recognize old behavior patterns, and address them when they arose. In addition, she had to reconnect with loyalty, respect, and trust in others. Most importantly, she learned to rebuild her self-worth and understand she was deserving of a better life. Robyn said this traumatic experience led her to her beautiful daughters, her now-husband, the love of her life, and their blended family.

Her message of hope is to not suffer in silence. Speak up, confide in someone, search for support groups and assistance programs, and, most importantly, report the abuse. She says one of her mistakes was never reporting. At court, the judge questioned how bad the situation could have been or how unsafe she truly felt because she never bothered to report the abuse. She countered with the fact that her abuser told her, "By the time the police showed up, you would be dead." Robyn learned the importance of reporting abuse and not making excuses for bad behaviour.

She also shared it is valuable to believe you deserve more and a better life is possible. Have a plan, envisage a future, dare to dream, build an emergency fund, and empower yourself with a career and education. Pray and reflect often. You are strong enough to leave the situation because you deserve a better life. There is light at the end of the tunnel, and although it sometimes feels like that light may be an oncoming train, it's not. So, stay strong, and remember you are not alone.

When I found out about Robyn's struggle, I decided to become her ray of light. I boarded a flight from Cape Town to be with my friend and hold space for her and the girls.

In both these stories, the decision to leave was challenging because it was complicated by the situation's complexity, abuse, and toxic environment. Having been brave enough to choose to go and live a different life, I often get asked why I stayed as long as I did. Truthfully, I was confined by the feeling a better life was not possible, which is true, I think, for many people who find themselves in similar situations. I wondered often if I could be a whole person without him and who could possibly love someone as broken as me. Would I be enough to exist on my own? Could I have conversations with others, considering he finished my sentences? Weighing up the different outcomes to leave always ended with the fear of "what if." What if it does not work out, what if I am alone, what if I can't pay my bills, what if I am not as good as I think I am, what if nobody loves me, what if I can't find happiness? I would overthink every one of the options that did not present a good outcome and eventually convince myself staying was not so bad and the cycle would continue.

I was curious to know why I was overthinking something that would be good for me and then convincing myself otherwise. I found making a decision while overthinking can be paralyzing. In the article "Decision Paralysis: How to stop overthinking your choices," the inability to choose is known as decision paralysis, or choice or analysis paralysis, and it is an insidious enemy. The article said decision paralysis occurs when we have to select from complicated options to compare. This paralysis is especially true when all the outcomes are plagued with what-ifs and are not favorable.

The more important or complex the choice, the more energy we must use to make the analysis. Having to choose creates negative emotions, which can lead to decision fatigue or a delay in making the decision. In many cases, even if a decision is made, decision paralysis exhausts the decision-maker so much they don't have any energy left to act itself.

Over the years, I learned choice is an essential part of life, and making choices for ourselves is a requirement for joy and inner peace. A difficult choice that both Robyn and I made for the better was to leave to find self-worth, self-love, freedom, joy, and inner peace. The choice is the doorway to greatness, and what we don't choose to change remains the same. Only we have the power to do something about our circumstances. I now know to always choose life from a place of hope, not fear.

CHAPTER FOUR:

GRIEF AND LOSS

"Grieving doesn't make you imperfect. It makes you human."
—SARAH DESSEN

When we think about grief and loss, we think of it in the context of the loss of a loved one, but grief can affect so many other areas of our lives. We have witnessed how the worldwide COVID-19 pandemic crisis left so much death and terror in its wake. As the pandemic unfolded, it provoked fear, anxiety, stress, tension, sadness, and sorrow, and we entered collective grief globally.

During the pandemic, many people were confronting the loss of a loved one to the coronavirus, and it was made even more difficult because of the physical distancing orders. This changed the way we say goodbye to our loved ones because we couldn't be with them or start our grieving process at the funeral to gather with others to mourn. According to a March 2021 *Washington Post* article by Cathy Alter, Ted Rynearson, a clinical professor of psychiatry at the University of Washington, said, "We are narrative- and meaning-seeking creatures." A death from COVID-19 tells its particular tale. "The dying story is one of isolation," Rynearson said. "The family can't say goodbye in a natural and private interchange. They can't hold one another—or be with one another at the time of death. They may be unable to separate themselves from the traumatic story of the way that their loved one died." There is, Rynearson said, "no pill for this. No medicine that helps with grief."

At the same time, people were also faced with other losses, giving up daily routines, loss of employment, and financial upheaval because of the pandemic. So, overall, people who haven't lost a stable job, income, or a loved one were now also grieving because the loss of a routine, which may not previously have been viewed as a loss worth grieving. According to a June 2020 American Psychological Association article by Kirsten Weir, Robert Neimeyer, PhD, director of the Portland Institute for Loss and Transition and professor emeritus of psychology at the University of Memphis, said, "Of course, we aren't only attached to other humans. We're capable of losing places, projects, possessions, professions, and protections, all of which we may be powerfully attached to. This pandemic forces us to confront the frailty of such attachments, whether it's to our local bookstore or the routines that sustain us through our days."

Neimeyer goes on to explain that many of the losses we're experiencing now are so-called ambiguous losses. "These lack the clarity and definition of a single point like a death," Neimeyer explains. That fuzziness can make it hard to move forward. As the pandemic has evolved, people have had to confront a series of losses: the loss of a sense of safety, of social connections and personal freedoms, of jobs and financial security. In the future, people will experience new losses we can't yet predict. "We're talking about grieving a living loss—one that keeps going and going."

We don't only grieve for what's missing, but also for how those losses affect our sense of self, said George Bonanno, PhD, a psychologist who heads the Loss, Trauma, and Emotion Lab at Teachers College, Columbia University: "You can experience grief over anything that feels like a loss of identity." Research shows, for instance, that losing a job can trigger a period of prolonged grief distinct from anxiety or depression. Moreover, prolonged grief seems to be related to the impacts of job loss on self-esteem and belief in a just world. This comes back to the shattered assumptions theory that challenges a person's belief system or worldview following a traumatic experience (2020).

According to a June 2020 "Grieving a living loss" article, Bonanno stated, "Grief is really about turning inward and recalibrating, and thinking: 'This is not the way the world is anymore, and I need to adapt.'" So, going through a traumatic experience, we will need to grieve to cope with the loss. However, grief can also be transient; even when we are in the midst of its clutches, it is okay to feel sad and happy. It's okay to cry, yet allow yourself to be distracted and laugh. Learning to adapt is exactly what Laura Thomas experienced on her healing journey following grief and loss.

Laura Thomas in a TEDx Talk shared how she dealt with her grief after her brother Scott took his life. Following this tragic event, she felt herself being thrown into a world of grief she knew nothing about. She shared that she was ill-equipped to navigate this new reality because there weren't only those expected experiences of grief, sorrow, heartache, and desperately wishing for life to be different. Other experiences felt harder to describe, even a little bit shameful. But, when she was grieving, she found a greater capacity to love herself and others, and since her brother no longer had his life, she felt this newfound gratitude for hers, like grief made her feel more alive. Experiencing this grief that was unknown, she realized she did not know how to talk or feel about it. So, she did what so many people do. She stuffed it way down deep inside, and she made grief this problem that she had to solve or get over.

I understood grief too; after all, I was grieving my own death. I was grieving the girl who died on the cold floor in a pool of blood and semen. That girl didn't get to go to the hospital but instead left in a body bag. I did not experience life the same as before, yet I was expected to fit into the life of that dead girl. I was expected to return to university, complete my degree, continue working at the restaurant, and even continue to date the same guy. To everyone else, my return to my life was a step in a positive direction. Resuming my life meant I must be healing, right? No, it was more complicated than that. I no longer belonged to that life and returning made me feel completely disconnected.

I felt stuck in a world that no longer made sense to me. I wondered why I only died metaphorically and not physically. Why was I stuck in a life that felt like it was not mine? I questioned why was I spared only to suffer like this. During my therapy sessions, we unpacked these questions because I needed to make sense of this new reality. What was it that made me feel this way? I heard my psychologist say grief and I immediately thought, *But I am not crying.* Over the days, weeks, and months that followed, I pondered the grief I was experiencing. I thought grief was reserved for a loss like death, but here I was, alive. I was feeling so sad and empty, and my heart was breaking so bad as I grieved what could have been and who I would have become.

Just like Laura, I did not want to feel this grief. I wanted to fast forward through it or stuff it down. I started to avoid my emotions and I overreacted to small things in my life because I felt like it was not supposed to be that way. Everything that happened was right or wrong. I always looked at it through the lens of a life lost. This made living in my reality very difficult because grief took over my life and consumed me. Finally, I reached my breaking point and I cried, something I had not been able to do since that horrible day.

I also understood grief from the perspective of the loss of a loved one, many years before I watched my parents push their emotions deep inside and try to solve their grief by searching for answers. In December 1994, my family and I grieved the loss of a brother. My brother was a natural leader, a dependable big brother, an awesome sibling, and a wonderful son to my parents. He devoted his life to the upliftment of others, but this noble act had dire consequences for him. He passed away at age thirty on December 6, 1994. This was the year South Africa held its first democratic election in April 1994 under an interim Constitution in a government of national unity under President Mandela, South Africa's first democratically elected president. Times were changing, and being a leader and educator, my brother deemed it fit to run for mayor of his hometown. As a teacher, he had contact with the parents of the students in his class, of whom the majority were farmworkers. Through his work and his campaign, he took on the topic of the dop system. According to "The Ramification of the South African Dop System," the dop system was one in which employers paid their laborers with cheap wine, or dops. My brother did not support this system and decided to educate farmworkers in the area about the disadvantages and negative consequences of the dop system, including alcohol abuse and human rights.

Today, the dop system is no longer legal in South Africa, but alcoholism remains one of the major challenges facing health services in the Western Cape. Even after the banishment of the dop system, alcohol dependency among farm workers continued to play a major role in trapping the farm workers in a cycle of poverty and dependence. According to South African History online, communities report of alcohol-related trauma, exceptionally high rates of TB, child and adult malnutrition, and fetal alcohol syndrome are common in the Western Cape. In addition, social problems associated with alcohol, including child abuse, violence against women, and family disruption, are major obstacles to health and social services for farm residents.

My brother was a determined young man who believed in a cause, and that was not liked or accepted by many in and around the town where he lived. He had also taken on a case of an evicted farm worker and was due to act as the representative at court the following week on December 9. On December 4, we had a wonderful family dinner arranged by my brother, and at the end of the evening, my Dad raised concerns because during that week there had been rumors of his impending murder and my brother had received death threats. His reply was, "Dad, if they kill me, there will be another to rise instead of me." Two days later, on December 6, at approximately 2:00 a.m., we received the news. My brother had been involved in a single motor vehicle accident just outside the town. Passersby called the ambulance, but it took them two hours to arrive. He lay in the field and bled out. Later that morning, my father and younger brother made the dreaded trip to the morgue to identify his body. A smaller trauma within a bigger trauma. Following a police investigation into the suspicious death and the opening of an official inquest, it was found to be inconclusive.

After this tragic and violent death, our family was in shock because we never expected to lose a son, brother, father, and husband. The pain was so bad I do not think any of us could breathe. Every thought was connected to our eyeballs, and with every thought, tears streamed down our faces. The idea of not seeing our brother again left a massive void in our lives. This was especially true for me because I was not only experiencing grief and loss of a big brother, but I was also watching my parents struggle with the grief of the loss of their son, being unable to let go of the desperate need for answers explaining the past and the anguish of living a life without him in the future.

My parents grieved differently. I watched my dad search for answers, and for the next five years he was obsessed with getting the truth. My mom became disconnected: She retreated within, she stopped talking, and she cried often. As I watched her, I learned that on her silent days, she missed my brother just a little louder. One parent spoke about the events all the time, the other was silent. I watched as my parents became lost in their grief. This traumatic experience had once again shattered our worldview, the belief in a benevolent world, where it had meaning, where it was just and orderly and parents did not outlive their children.

According to the 1998 article "Coping with loss: Bereavement in adult life," three main components affect the process of grieving. They include the urge to look back, cry, and search for what is lost, and the conflicting urge to look forward, explore the world that now emerges, and discover what can be carried forward from the past. Overlying these are the social and cultural pressures that influence how the urges are expressed or inhibited. The strength of these urges varies greatly and changes over time, giving rise to constantly changing reactions.

My dad's way of coping was to look back and launch an investigation that led him to numerous conclusions about the circumstances surrounding my brother's death. After much research, my father concluded my brother had been murdered by a Third Force group that operated in the area. Despite being aware of who the perpetrators are, proving it in court will be a challenge. My dad found comfort in the fact had he raised a son who was a respected member of the community who devoted his life to stand up for the oppressed against an inherently oppressive system that contributed in its own way to the fall of the apartheid system in South Africa. In the little town, my brother was honored for his bravery, and the major named a street after him.

My mom found her comfort in the love of family and a community that loved her son. The days, weeks, months, and years that followed were filled with family and friends that brought love, understanding, and compassion. It eventually allowed my mom to start opening up and talk about her grief, and through her tears, she let go of her emotions. She spoke to other families who lost children and learned how they navigated their grief, which in turn helped her make sense of her own. The many visits to spend time with my mom and with us was a big part of helping my mom and my family through the grieving process.

Both my parents found ways to learn to live with the loss in the present moment as opposed to the past, and they found new meaning and purpose in life. As they healed and the grief started to change, my parents started to include their other children in their healing journey, which helped us to feel part of the family unit once again. As a family, we started to find new ways of remembering my brother and honoring his life, and that brought us joy and inner peace. We understood our grief was a sign of the big love we have for our brother. We learned to hold onto the love, not the loss.

Laura says there is the subtle grief of being gifted this moment, this precious gem of an experience, and in an instant, it's gone, never to be reclaimed because we can't hold on to life; it keeps slipping through our fingers. So in some ways, big and small grief colors all of life.

In her talk, she offered three recommendations for when nothing you have tried is working any longer and you feel overwhelmed by grief. The first is to allow grief to be present and remember it is not a sign you are broken. It's not a sign something needs to be fixed or gotten over; it is a normal human experience. She says we grieve big because we love big, and we're equipped to feel both. Secondly, she recommends we be gentle with ourselves during the grieving process because sometimes we can be so hard and demanding on ourselves, but grief doesn't respond to demands or to-do lists or timelines. It has its meandering journey, and the best way to allow grief to unfold is to be gentle. Lastly, she recommends you find someone you love, someone you trust, and ask them to be with you, not to fix you, not to make you feel different or better, but to sit with you and let you know you're not alone.

Laura says when it comes to grief, we don't have a way of talking about it. We make grief a part of our collective experience, so we stuff it deep inside. For some people, this avoidance works; for others, it only works for a while, and it can even become harmful. According to the 2012 "Grief and Mourning Gone Awry" article, most adults do not wander the streets crying aloud for a dead person. Bereaved people often try to avoid reminders of the loss and to suppress the expression of grief. What emerges is a compromise, a partial expression of feelings that are experienced as arising compellingly and illogically from within.

The article continues and stated much empirical evidence supports the claims of the psychoanalytic school that excessive repression of grief is harmful and can give rise to delayed and distorted grief—but there is also evidence that obsessive grieving, to the exclusion of all else, can lead to chronic grief and depression.

The ideal is to achieve a balance between avoidance and confrontation, which enables the person to gradually come to terms with the loss. Until people have gone through the painful process of searching, they cannot "let go" of their attachment to the lost person and move on to review and revise their basic assumptions about the world. A shattered worldview needs to be restored. This process, which has been termed psychosocial transition, is similar to the relearning that takes place when a person becomes disabled or loses a body part.

For Laura, repressing her emotions inside felt like she couldn't bring her whole self to her life anymore. She describes it was like there was this part of her that she had deemed acceptable and normal and was predictable, and this other part felt shaky and vulnerable, and sometimes a little broken, so she became half a person straddling worlds. Being torn in this way was taxing, and she reached a point where she no longer wanted that for herself, this half-life, and clearly, her brother would not want this for her either. So in dealing with her grief, Laura decided to bring her grief to the stage in the form of a one-woman play that she wrote and produced and performed in, and she brought all her questions and curiosities and joys and pains. She found a place to start the conversation, and she would ask the audience to discuss this topic with her afterward. In doing so, she created an experience where grief felt normalized, as they could connect over it.

The discussions with the audience allowed for grief not to feel overwhelming. Still, through sharing and discussion, they grieved together, because nobody's grief was too big for that group to hold together. Everybody in the audience had their own stories and backgrounds, but there was something fundamental about their experience of grief, something that felt shared. Through coming together around it, she says it felt like they could heal a little bit together.

Laura says there are no right or wrong words for those who wish to support someone. Everybody's so different, and grief changes over time. However, if someone is grieving, you could say to them, "I am so sorry for your loss, for your pain." You could say, "I see you. I hear you, and I choose you, just as you are." You could say, "I don't know what to say right now, but I'd like to be here with you while you're grieving. I want to hold your hand as you cross that threshold, because maybe what's on the other side isn't so scary or uncomfortable or even painful if you and I go together." For the loved ones of those grieving, I agree with Laura's advice. It also made me think of the words of author Gerard Long, whom I spoke to on my podcast, *Surviving Trauma: Stories of Hope*. He calls it the ministries of presence. He recommends to come alongside the bereaved party and tell them you are there for them, you love them, and you pray for them if you are a person of faith during this period of comfort.

In general, we have all had an encounter with grief and have had the opportunity to walk with it. She explained we don't only experience grief through the loss of a loved one. We also experience grief when life doesn't go the way we want. For example, we experience grief in losing a friendship or a dream or waking up to how hard we can be on ourselves. Sometimes we experience grief when we have an illness, injury, or when there's injustice. We can even experience ecological, political, and social grief. Her description of this type of grief resonated with me because I have experienced this kind of grief through following the attempted murder on my life years after my brother's death.

As we have seen, grief is usually associated with the loss of a loved one and the loss of places, protections, routines, identity, and our sense of self. When someone talks about sexual assault, rape, attempted murder, serious illness, dreaded disease, or divorce, one rarely thinks to associate the traumatic event with the concept of grief and loss. However, when survivors consider their pain and the trauma they have experienced, the idea of going through the stages of grief may never cross their minds. After a traumatic event, we as survivors of sexual violence may need to mourn the loss of our identity, the loss of our "normal" life held before the traumatic experience, or even, in cases when victims know their abuser, the loss of their abuser as a person they once had in their life. Grief is part of the healing journey, and, in my experience, without intention, I used the five-stage grief model to navigate the deep pain and loss that came with surviving rape and attempted murder.

The renowned Swiss psychiatrist Elizabeth Kübler-Ross first introduced her five-stage grief model in her book, *On Death and Dying*. Her grief model was based on her work with terminally ill patients. In the beginning, it was not readily accepted because many mistakenly thought people had to go through all the stages of grief. However, Kübler-Ross now notes these stages are not linear, and some people may not experience any of them. So, it is possible to go through some of the stages and not others, or people can go through all five stages of grief.

According to Kübler-Ross, the five stages include denial, anger, bargaining, depression, and acceptance. During my trauma recovery, I experienced all five stages of grief. The denial stage initially helped me survive the loss of a life I had before someone tried to murder me. It was easier to avoid thinking and feeling the emotions attached with the trauma. Like Laura, I pushed my emotions deep inside, and I did not like when a situation like talking to my psychologist caused a disturbance on my spiritual heart. I would feel this disturbance when my psychologist would invite conversation about the trauma. It was a shut door in my mind that I avoided for a long time.

Anger about my experience was an easy emotion to succumb to during the anger stage. I was angry at the world and everyone in it, starting with God for letting this heinous act happen to me. I had to live in "actual" reality again and not in my "preferable" reality. Finally, I became outraged, and I started to think, *Why me?* and *Life's not fair!* I found it incomprehensible something like this could happen to me. I was grieving a life lost, and I was so desperate to get my life back to how it was before that in the bargaining stage, I was willing to make a deal with God if He would make life just a little easier. I was plagued with what-ifs. What if I was not so angry? God, could you take this heavy burden from my shoulders? If I am not so pissed off, could you make the thoughts stop? But it felt like God could not hear me, and it made me angrier.

During the depression stage, I started to withdraw from life. I felt numb, living every day in a haze. Facing the world was too much and too overwhelming. I remember telling my dad

I wanted to lie in the corner of the world and die. He said, "I understand how you feel, but for now, you must find the courage to face the world again. We do not understand why certain things happen to us, but one day we will look back and understand." I took my dad's words of encouragement and guidance and braved the world armed with courage and antidepressants. I didn't feel like talking, and the experience left me feeling hopeless. Yet, somehow, I manage to pull myself out of bed every day and build a life after trauma.

During the acceptance stage of my grief, my emotions began to stabilize as I accepted what had happened, and I had the willingness to accept my new reality. I was changed. Trauma changes us, and it is what you do in your new reality that matters. It took a long time to adjust and readjust, but my good days eventually outweighed the bad days.

Through the process of grief and loss, I learned repressed emotions have a place, and it can be a normal reaction to a trauma experience, whatever that may be. It is important not to stay in that space but to move from repression to processing and release or letting go. The themes highlighted through these stories are to feel your emotions, search outward then inward for answers to make sense of your new world, engage in interconnected healing with others who have similar experiences, be kind and gentle with yourself, and embrace life from a place of gratitude. While the five stages of grief have been shown to represent the process of grief for many, it is important to realize grief is an individualized experience that is different for everyone. Not all individuals grieve in the same way; some may progress quickly through some stages, and others may take a long period of time. Healing from a sexual trauma or any traumatic experience occurs differently for each survivor, but in my experience, it is not a quick process, and the same goes for working through the five stages of grief. What I do know for sure is that with a strong network of support, time, and a willingness to heal, survivors can find their way toward acceptance and live a life of joy and inner peace.

CHAPTER FIVE:

RELIGION AND SPIRITUALITY

"Religion helps us create a space for God, but it is through spirituality that we can find God inside and outside of any defined spaces."

—TOYIN OMOFOYE

When tragedy strikes, it is a normal reaction to question faith and have doubts, as Greg Tonkinson shared with the audience in a TEDx Talk called "Faith and Doubt." Greg described a rather uninteresting Saturday evening at home with his children that was interrupted by a knock at the door. Upon opening the door, he was met by a police officer, a child caseworker, and a police chaplain. That same evening, their lives changed when he was notified that at approximately 7:45 p.m. that evening, his wife, Leigh Ann, had been killed in a motor vehicle accident. Leigh Ann was at a stoplight two miles from her home when she was hit from behind. The best they could tell was that her neck was broken on impact, making her passing immediate and painless. After delivering the death notification to Greg, the officer sympathized with his loss.

On March 6, 2010, Greg and his three children began their journey through life without their wife and mother. He described a journey of grief that was plagued by an assortment of emotions, such as feelings of rage, anger, joy, hopelessness, frustration, and even moments of serenity. At his core, he describes himself as a man of faith, a faith that has defined him, his occupation, his academic qualifications, and the way he raises his children for over thirty years. All have faith at their nucleus. Over the days and weeks that followed, Greg questioned, What do you do when your faith has been traumatized by a traumatic event? What do you do when your identity has been rolled up in a worldview that promotes blessing and favor? What do you do when you told people to trust, follow, and obey? What do you do when you start to doubt the subject that you have promoted for your entire life?

In these moments, he had grievances that he levied against God Almighty, doubting God's plan. He wondered whether you could maintain a healthy relationship with God while expressing and experiencing your doubt. Faith and doubt will forever be linked, and those who don't doubt are not experiencing faith. After much deliberation and soul searching, he arrived at this conclusion: perhaps the reason we doubt is not that we are seeking answers or expressing raw emotion but to change minds. Doubting God allowed him to believe he had some control. The doubting allowed Greg to go to God and question God's plan and present his own plan following Leigh Ann's death.

He said the exhilaration of doubting God was replaced with a serious decision that he had to make somewhere along the line. That decision was that either God was in control of his trials and tragedies, or that God wasn't in control, and He would forever put up with his doubting and speculating and even change the course of history based on his suggestions. However, if that's the case, then he said, "Is it not true that higher power, by definition, ceases to be just that—a higher power—but instead is reduced to a glorified peer with a much cooler title?" This peace he had known due to his faith for over thirty years was being eroded, and he wanted it back.

This realization brought him to a significant crossroads. He was either going to spend his remaining days doubting God's plan, or he was going to spend his remaining days doing his plan. Both options, he admitted, were imperfect, confusing, and messy, but he had a choice to make, and he chose the latter. Part of that plan was to start using Leigh Ann's death for good.

Leigh Ann's death was not unique, he realized as he talked to many people who had gone through a tragedy. At his wife's funeral, he was greatly encouraged to see how many people's faith increased after listening to how she lived her life here. She has even had several children named after her. He takes great pride in knowing that when those kids grow up and ask their moms and dads where their name came from, his wife will be mentioned in that conversation.

Leigh Ann's best friend, Andra Good, started an international nonprofit. Leigh Ann was a pediatric nurse, and now thousands of children's blankets are going all over the world helping little ones in need. Since then, he remarried and has embarked on a journey with his wife and stepmother to his children. However, he said he continues to doubt, but he likes to believe his doubting is framed for the way that Jesus Christ framed his uncertainties that night before the cross when he went to God with his concerns. But in the end, he asked for God's will, not his own. However, Greg admits that he often does not possess that kind of strength.

He acknowledges that wondering why this happened will always be a part of his journey. However, he has landed on the side of this discussion that promotes asking God for wisdom instead of doubting Him. But to let him readily admit that not only is it honest to doubt something that should be expected when someone goes through tragedy in some paradoxical way, but doubting can increase one's faith, as he has experienced just that. Tragedy is universal; we are in this together. Perhaps we would be better served if we opened spaces free of judgment for people to share their aches and anguish and agonies regardless of a religious disposition. He said there is incredible power in understanding and empathizing with people who are in pain and suggested we rejoice and weep together, and may we do it well.

Again, when tragedy strikes, our religious and spiritual beliefs are impacted, and we want to make sense of it to feel better and find purpose, peace, and well-being. Hundreds of studies have investigated the relationship between religious involvement and mental health (Peres et al, 2007). In most cases, they have found higher levels of religious involvement are associated with greater well-being and mental health following a traumatic experience. Positive religious coping has been associated not only with better physical and mental outcomes in medically ill patients but also among trauma survivors such as people affected by large-scale floods.

According to the "11 ways to cultivate resilience" article on *PsychCentral* April 5, 2018, religion and spirituality have been shown to predict resilience in various populations studied, including returning war veterans with posttraumatic stress disorder, trauma sufferers, children and adults who experience abuse or violence, and patients enduring chronic pain. In addition, prayer, self-reflection, and communicating with a Higher Power serves as a healing balm to many who otherwise may resort to negative coping behaviors. However, religious coping is not always related to better outcomes, because we do experience negative religious coping, for example, when we start to doubt and question whether God had abandoned us. In this particular two-year longitudinal study, negative religious coping in ill elderly patients was associated with increased mortality as opposed to positive religious coping that has been associated with better physical and mental outcomes.

As a trauma survivor, I experienced both negative and positive religious coping, and they were both normal trauma responses. After the attack, I wondered why a loving God would allow this to happen, and I doubted God's plan for me. My traumatic experience and the consequences thereof weakened my religious and spiritual faith, but it propelled me on a quest to find meaning and purpose. First, I was led to a place of doubt, then eventually to a place of acceptance and understanding. This search allowed me to cope with the aftermath of my trauma.

During my research, I came across a study that reviewed eleven empirical studies of associations between religion, spirituality, and posttraumatic growth that reported three main findings. Firstly, religion and spirituality are usually, although not always, beneficial in dealing with the aftermath of trauma; secondly, traumatic experiences may lead to a deepening of religiousness or spirituality; and lastly, positive religious coping, religious openness, readiness to face existential questions, religious participation, and intrinsic religiousness were typically associated with posttraumatic growth.

In the study, Kenneth Pargament proposed religious coping may have something unique to offer: "It may uniquely equip individuals to respond to situations in which they come face-to-face with the limits of human power and control and are confronted with their vulnerability and finitude." Religious beliefs and practices may reduce loss of control and helplessness, provide a cognitive framework that can decrease suffering, and strengthen one's purpose and meaning in the face of trauma. Religion can also provide a worldview that helps give purpose and meaning to despair, besides hope and motivation.

The concept of religious coping involves several cognitive aspects and some examples of positive religious coping, including benevolent reappraisal such as seeking a lesson from God in the event and seeking spiritual support by searching for comfort and reassurance through God's love and care. Active religious surrender can include doing what one can and then putting the rest in God's hands, seeking spiritual connection by thinking about how life is part of a more significant spiritual force, and seeking religious direction by praying to find a new reason to live. A religious or spiritual belief system helps interpret life events and give them meaning and coherence, which may contribute to the psychological integration of traumatic experiences.

Through this journey, I learned that I wanted to understand more deeply the similarities and differences between religion and spirituality, because I often have seen the words used interchangeably. According to a *Religion, Spirituality and Health* paper,

Religion is a multidimensional construct that includes beliefs, behaviors, rituals, and ceremonies that may be held or practiced in private or public settings but are in some way derived from established traditions that developed over time within a community. Religion is also an organized system of beliefs, practices, and symbols designed (a) to facilitate closeness to the transcendent, and (b) to foster an understanding of one's relationship and responsibility to others in living together in a community.

Spirituality is distinguished from all other things, like humanism, values, morals, and mental health but by its connection to that which is sacred, the *transcendent*. The transcendent is that which is outside of the self, and yet also within the self. Spirituality includes both a search for the transcendent and the discovery of the transcendent and so involves traveling along the path that leads from non-consideration to questioning to either staunch nonbelief or belief, and if belief, then ultimately to devotion and finally, surrender.

Religious beliefs and spirituality provide many people with a vital context of meaning for life's events. However, for most trauma survivors, the events often call into question the foundation of their faith. For me, as a trauma survivor, this became an issue of ongoing significance. When I started talking about my faith positively and accepting the experiences had happened not to me but for me, I found meaning in the pain and suffering. I understood my pain in the larger scheme of things was necessary for my self-sustenance and self-growth.

When I was young, I dreamed about being a children's television presenter sharing stories and playing fun games on the afternoon show. I wanted to leave an impact on the lives of the viewers. Even at that young age, I had an innate sense I had a story to share. This innate sense, an intuition, would stay with me and would serve as gentle reminders throughout my life. Coming from a conservative Christian family and being the youngest sibling, my parents were not going to let me set my sails for the big city at the tender age of nine to become a television star. Despite being part of a wonderfully loving family with parents and siblings who adored me, I was exposed to several traumatic events throughout my life, each bringing lessons with it. I would spend most of my life processing and recovering from my traumas while living a seemingly happy life.

A life that seemed perfect and shiny from the outside.

Many years later, on Friday the thirteenth, I was diagnosed with cancer. The Monday before the diagnosis, with a light and happy heart, I decided to pay a visit to my spiritual medium. I could feel that the Spirit world had a message, and I was ready to listen. As we opened with a prayer, calling on God to help us connect with those who wished to step forward and communicate with messages I could use practically, my heart was full. I remember feeling centered and connected to God. It was one of the first times in my life when I did not seek from a place of desperation but was ready to listen from a place of empowerment.

The messages came, "You have free radicals in your body. It is going to be okay; let go and allow Spirit Divine to hold you. Internal conflict will make things worse. Find your anchor." Knowing I had the blessing from God and the love and support from everyone in the spirit world, I was fearless as I stepped into the valley of the shadow of death. There was no religious or spiritual traumatization, only gratitude for a Merciful and Graceful God. The difference now was I engaged in positive religious and spiritual coping that led me to pay attention to the message that my dreaded disease brought.

The familiar and recurring themes of healing and recovery I had been dealing with for years became prominent throughout my cancer journey. As I listened with my heart and my gut, I embraced the virtue, the gift from my cancer. Armored with this newly discovered courage, I decided to choose my life and honor my old friend, the gentle reminder from my soul to live my life's purpose and find the meaning in my suffering. In the years that followed, I started to make notes for my book in preparation for the opportunity that would inevitably arrive. All the while, I stayed grounded in my religion and spirituality and asked God to guide me every step of the way.

On the evening of December 21, 2020, I asked God for a sign that would confirm my purpose of owning my story and sharing it in a meaningful way that would touch lives and bring hope to many. Later that evening, my pup woke me up for his midnight walk. We walked all around as he sniffed away to find the perfect place for his wee, and as he positioned himself for the long-awaited release, I decided to marvel at the stars. At that moment, as I looked up at the midnight sky, a barn owl gliding above turned and looked me in the face, a once-in-a-lifetime moment that I will never forget. I felt emotions rush through my body as I watched the owl glide over the three-story building against the backdrop of the moon. The moment brought a cosmic connection, a sense of inspiration to do new things with conviction, and confirmation to always have faith. I had my answer, and in the months that followed, I launched my podcast, *Surviving Trauma: Stories of Hope*, and commenced writing this book. Religious beliefs and spiritual practice once again helped me find meaning and purpose in the face of trauma.

Throughout my research, I discovered this is not unique to me, but many people all over the world have used religion and spirituality to cope and make sense of their experiences. In the book *Sexual Abuse in the Lives of Women Diagnosed with Serious Mental Illness*, through anonymous interviews, one woman said, "God created me not to suffer, but with what He feels we need to be, what He wants us to be . . . to develop strengths and accept weaknesses. . . . I can say I know who I am." Another woman who had been a victim of childhood physical abuse and sexual abuse in adulthood recalled thinking, "Why is this happening?" and concluding, "The Lord will put us through trials . . . kind of a learning experience, a strengthening." This has helped me to help others. Different religious and spiritual perspectives may consider these explanations differently, but for these individuals, they developed a clear idea of God's greater purpose in permitting their suffering, a purpose often difficult to fathom. It has enabled them to place their experiences in a meaningful perspective and has enhanced the possibility of recovery.

While researching and talking to many people about coping with and processing their trauma in the context of religion and spirituality, I was pleasantly surprised by the use of religious and spiritual rituals to cope and process traumatic experiences. One such ritual is the use of ayahuasca. According to "Introducing Ayahuasca," an article on the *Psychology Today* site, ayahuasca is a psychedelic traditional plant medicine that has been imbued with spiritual and psychological healing properties. Though ayahuasca was traditionally used for religious and spiritual purposes by specific populations, it has become popular worldwide among those who seek a way to open their minds, heal from past traumas, or simply experience an ayahuasca journey. It's strongly recommended that ayahuasca only be taken when supervised by an experienced shaman, as those who take it need to be looked after carefully, because an ayahuasca trip leads to an altered state of consciousness that lasts for many hours.

According to "The Ayahuasca Phenomenon" study published by the *Multidisciplinary Association for Psychedelic Studies*, to understand the ayahuasca ceremony, one must understand the role of the shaman in Indian and other societies of indigenous peoples. The word "shaman" comes from the Siberian Tungusic word for the person in a tribe of indigenous people who uses a type of magic to heal, foresee future events, and communicate with spirits, plants, animals, and other worlds. Shamans are most often male and are also called medicine men, witch doctors, curanderos, *vegetalistas*, and other names. Shamans either receive a "calling" to their role, or they can be chosen by others. They are chosen based on their knowledge, spiritual gifts, sensibility, relationship to other shamans, or some uniqueness or strangeness about them. Sometimes the shaman is reluctant to accept the role because of the physically demanding nature of the duties, but the spirit world does not let him rest until he accepts.

The shaman's job is to journey into the spirit world, or nonordinary reality, getting advice and powers to maintain the balance between the natural and supernatural. Shamans most commonly accomplish this journey by altering their consciousness through ritual methods such as drumming, dancing, chanting, and/or the use of psychotropic plants. In the Amazon, Indian shamans use chanting and plants such as those that make ayahuasca achieve this altered state.

Since journeys into nonordinary reality such as those achieved through the use of ayahuasca can be frightening, confusing, and dangerous, shamans help others with their journey. They prepare the candidates through strict diets, purging, and other rituals. The actual ceremony requires just the right location and site preparation, meaning the setting is critical to the quality of the experience.

I wanted to understand the ayahuasca ceremony firsthand and was fortunate enough to meet and sit down with CarmenMaria Navarro. She shared with me her experience of the spiritual ritual of ayahuasca and meditation used as a form of spiritual coping to open her mind and heal from past traumas and access positive, long-term, life-altering changes. Navarro, originally from Peru, explained that the tradition and ceremony surrounding this sacred plant medicine go back hundreds, maybe even thousands, of years. She shares that her friend was about to attend an ayahuasca ceremony and decided to invite her at the last minute. She was surprised yet excited and willing to try the new experience. Before participating in an ayahuasca ceremony, as mentioned before, it is recommended participants abstain from cigarettes, drugs, alcohol, sex, spicy food, red meat, and caffeine to purify their bodies. These are clear rules ahead of the ceremony, but since CarmenMaria was invited last minute, she had no time to observe these recommendations.

It is accepted that during these ceremonies, those who take ayahuasca can experience symptoms like vomiting, diarrhea, feelings of euphoria, strong visual and auditory hallucinations, mind-altering psychedelic effects, fear, and paranoia. When CarmenMaria arrived, shamans were leading the ayahuasca ceremony in a group setting that typically takes place over some time. She was given a mat and a bucket and the ayahuasca to consume. Throughout the evening, shamans sing chants, which describe the movement of spirits or energies during the ceremony. She said she started to feel the effects of the ayahuasca after approximately thirty minutes.

She describes she was hit with a wave of nausea followed by violent vomiting almost immediately. This was shortly followed by bouts of diarrhea. She lay on her mat, which seemed to alleviate some of the nausea. She was aware of her surroundings and the sounds of nature and others who were enduring the same experience. As the night progressed, the ayahuasca ritual became a very personal experience. She described the psychedelic experience as intense. She told me that during the hours that followed, she encountered characters, versions of herself. The initial experience was plagued by fear and uncertainty, but eventually she reached a place of calmness where she could question the "monsters" in her experience. As this was her first time, without mental preparation as to what she hoped to achieve, she had to allow herself to engage with the full experience of ayahuasca as it unfolded. For her, the messages that came through were to focus on forgiveness and self-love, something she needed in her life at that time. Slowly coming out of the experience after several hours, she felt connected to the universe, understood life differently, and felt connected to everyone who had undergone the experience with her. Since that time, Carmen Maria made use of the ayahuasca ritual several times as a form of spiritual and religious coping during challenging times. For the year that followed, she worked closely with the shaman using meditation to complete her healing.

Many Western governments have prohibited or persecuted those engaged in such practices. Still, there has been much effort by followers to gain legal use of ayahuasca in religious ceremonies. For example, in Peru and Brazil, several contemporary churches are based on the use of ayahuasca.

The need to make sense and find meaning in religion and spirituality for me continued over various religions and modalities. When I experienced a high vibrational frequency following trauma, the feeling was so intense and I felt so connected to God. I did not want to lose the feeling. Discussing this with my guru, she introduced me to the Hindu festival of Navratri and invited me to join the Garba.

According to the "Garba and Dandiya and Nivratri" article, Garba originated in Gujarat and is performed during Navratri. Why during Navratri? you may ask. The reason is these dance forms are a dramatization, sort of like a mock fight of the nine-day battle between goddess Durga and the demon king Mahishasura, in which the goddess emerged victoriously.

This is what Navratri symbolizes as well: the triumph of good over evil, even if that evil stems from our own cluttered and undisciplined minds. These nine days give us a chance to purify negative thoughts and remember all the good there is in the world. It helps us to reconnect the self to the Higher Power and start afresh. I participated in the Garba and learned and expressed all the dance variations. It was such an honor to participate in the Garba. Above all, in the Hindu community of Rylands, I found connectedness, healing, family, unity, and joy.

Religion and spirituality are not defined by only what we are prescribed to, but in our time of need they may be presented to us in the most unexpected places. Greg found it at the funeral, Carmen Maria found it in an invitation by a friend to join the ayahuasca ritual, and I found it at the Garba celebrating the Hindu festival of Navratri.

In conclusion, religion and spirituality have been central to trauma recovery and posttraumatic growth. Throughout all these special stories, everyone was looking for purpose and meaning following trauma. Many have found religion and spirituality can provide a worldview that helps give purpose and meaning to despair. There are many different ways to do that by using prayer, self-reflection, doing good for others, rituals like ayahuasca, or meditation to help facilitate the experience.

Religion and spirituality have not always been beneficial in dealing with the aftermath of trauma. Just like Greg, my religion and spirituality had been traumatized, and I chose to initially engage in negative coping strategies. Here, I want to emphasize that we always have a choice to make, and it shines through in the stories that were shared with me.

This theme that we have the power to choose was so strong. So, when I decided to adopt positive religious and spiritual coping strategies into my life, it improved my mental and physical well-being. It helped me make sense of what had happened, reduce my suffering, and strengthen the purpose and meaning of my life. During my spiritual awakening, I awakened to seek the lessons from God, I turned to God for comfort, and I learned to surrender. Just like Greg Tonkinson, I chose to turn my doubt into faith and use my traumatic experiences for good.

CHAPTER SIX:

FORGIVENESS

"Forgiveness is the gift you give yourself."

—TONY ROBBINS

In the summer of 2016, Sarah Montana said she did the sensible thing. She quit her job at a cushy hedge fund to write a play about her family's murder. She told friends and loved ones that this was about art, but Sarah was secretly on a spiritual vision quest seeking to close a relationship with a person she barely knew, the kid who killed her mother and brother. He was her friend's younger brother, a kid from their neighborhood, who came over a handful of times to raid their family snack cabinet. Her mom used to wave to him from the van and say, "He's going through a hard time. I want to make sure he knows that I see him."

This boy broke into their house a couple of days before Christmas, looking for some stuff to sell for cash. When he came across her brother Jim asleep on the couch, he panicked, shot him, and fled the scene. Then he realized he had forgotten his coat. By the time he came back to the house, Sarah's mom had found her brother, and because the boy knew

Sarah's mom recognized him and, quoting him, because "she wouldn't stop screaming," he shot and killed her too. He's currently serving back-to-back life sentences in a prison in southwest Virginia.

In dealing with her grief, Sarah said that over the next seven years she managed not to hate the boy, but her trauma did something weird: It made him a nonperson to her. He was the face of all evil, not a seventeen-year-old boy or the twenty-four-year-old man that came of age in a cell, if he came of age at all. According to Sarah, in her TEDx Talk, when she sat down to write the villain of the play and her life, she realized she had a name, fractured childhood memories, a brief court document, and nothing else to go on.

To find more information, she turned to Google and searched the prisoner ID number and was overwhelmed by the amount of human rights violations at the prison. Suddenly this boy became a person to her again. In that moment, Sarah recalled seeing her mother and brother at the morgue and witnessing the hole the bullet left in Jim's skull. Her mother's face had just collapsed in on itself. It was not her, she recalls, it was merely flesh and bones in the black dress that they had bought at Kohl's the week before. However, when she pictured the boy, her villain who was now a person again, beaten, starving, and crying out in a dark cell, she felt it was just as painful as seeing her mother and brother in the morgue. In that moment, as painful as it was, she started seeing the boy as human, and she realized they were still connected by that steel tether of trauma that he hooked into her side when he killed her mother and brother. It was still there. Over the prior seven years, she had been lurching against its pull—dragging the boy through the mud, whether she knew it or not. At that moment, she realized he may have killed them, but with a bit of horror, she realized she chose to keep them connected.

In the months leading up to the trial, I prepared myself for the testimony. I knew I would be asked many questions and I wanted to be prepared. I decided to write everything down because I did not want to forget any detail—an ironic twist considering all I wanted to do is forget.

I sat in a quiet hallway waiting to testify in the trial. Every now and then I heard the clanking of a door and footsteps either coming closer or fading. Diagonally opposite was accused number two, an accused-turned-state witness, or section 204 state witness, as it is known in the criminal justice system. This meant an accomplice testified despite the self-incriminatory nature of the testimony. Should the questions be answered frankly and honestly, the court could indemnify the witness from prosecution.

I heard the court orderly call my name, and as I stood up, I felt the weight of the steel tether weighing me down. As I entered the courtroom, the prosecutor came over to speak to me. I stared past him because I wanted my stare to let accused number one know, unequivocally, that I was here to seek justice and it was game on. Behind me, I heard a court reporter verbalize her interest in the case. "This is a story worth telling." I squirmed at the thought of this story on the front page of the newspaper.

I took the stand and was sworn in as a witness. The stand was high and, save for the magistrate, I had a bird's eye view of the courtroom. The prosecutor asked me to recall what happened on the day in question. I felt nervous sitting in the witness stand. I had to open the door in my mind I had shut months before. I knew opening that door was an act of bravery and a necessity. I slowly started recounting the events in a quiet courtroom with all eyes focused on me and all ears hanging onto my every word. I could feel my insides shaking as I spoke. As I testified, the accused laughed at me, but I knew I would have the last laugh.

Under cross-examination by the accused attorney, I was badgered, but I stood my ground. At the sentencing hearing, I was commended by the advocate for my thorough testimony. The highest sentence for the crimes was imposed. Justice served.

I had justice, but what was it about the trial coming to an end that left me thinking, *What now?* We somehow put our lives on hold as if the outcome of the trial would be a magic wand that could erase everything and make it so much better.

After wading through all the options, Sarah realized the only way to get rid of this boy was to forgive him. She giggled and shared there are sixty-two passages in the Bible that talk about forgiveness, and not a single one tells you how to do it. So, she asked herself why to forgive and realized most people forgive for the wrong reasons, but if we are honest about forgiveness, there are only three reasons we want to forgive automatically. One, we think forgiving quickly will make us a good person, but that's an easy mistake to make.

On her quest, she never could find a timeline for forgiveness; there was no appropriate time when it should happen that supported this notion of forgiving quickly. Two, it just seemed like everybody was urging her and the family along to forgive. She says victims generally feel a lot of pressure from everyone like friends, family, and even the media to forgive, but the truth is they want you to forgive so that they can feel more comfortable and so they can move on. Three, you think that to forgive is a shortcut to healing, a way to skip to the end of the story and you can bypass all the angry, vulnerable, messy healing that awaits.

Sarah asked, "Why forgive?" It can't heal you, save you, or make you a good person. Forgiveness is designed to set you free. When you say, "I forgive you," you mean, "I know what you did and it's not okay," or, "I don't want to hold us captive to this situation any longer and I want to heal." When we forgive, it is important to be clear about what we forgive. According to Sarah, in Judaism, a family cannot forgive a murderer because they were not killed. They can only forgive the pain, anguish, and grief the loss caused them. It is justice's job to assess what is owed to society, so when you are about to forgive, you have to be clear about what you are owed, and in real forgiveness, one has to let go of all expectations.

The first thing Sarah did was identify what was done to her and assess her damages. After all, if you don't know what happened to you, you can't understand what you're forgiving. When she decided to forgive, all the weight lifted off her and she found the girl inside that she had not seen in many years. Sarah said it's never too late to let go of your villains and reclaim yourself. If you're ready to let it all go—the grief, the pain, the anger, and the trauma—you will find out who you are.

According to an article in *Greater Good Magazine*, psychologists generally define forgiveness as a conscious, deliberate decision to release feelings of resentment or vengeance toward a person or group who has harmed you, regardless of whether they deserve your forgiveness. At the same time, it is crucial when defining what forgiveness *is* to understand what forgiveness is *not*. Experts who study or teach forgiveness clarify that when you forgive, you do not gloss over or deny the seriousness of an offense against you. Forgiveness does not mean forgetting, nor does it mean condoning or excusing crimes. Though forgiveness can help repair a damaged relationship, it doesn't obligate you to reconcile with the person who harmed you or release them from legal accountability. Instead, forgiveness brings the forgiver peace of mind and frees them from corrosive anger. Experts agree it at least involves letting go of deeply held negative feelings. In that way, it empowers you to recognize the pain you suffered without letting that pain define you, enabling you to heal and move on with your life.

Forgiveness has also been connected to improved health. Much research has shown forgiveness is linked to lower levels of anxiety and depression and is also associated with benefits in both physical and mental health, while not forgiving can raise heart rate and blood pressure. A study examining the relationship of forgiveness to pain, anger, and psychological distress further yielded that emotion mediates the relationship between forgiveness and chronic low back pain. Specifically, individuals who suffered from chronic low back pain experienced lower levels of sensory pain when they were more forgiving, and they stated anger mediated the relationship between forgiveness and sensory pain. In sum, forgiveness is associated with less harmful and more positive aspects of physical and mental health.

Holding onto negative emotions from the past can feel like a source of comfort and form part of who we are; it is the glue that holds us together. The idea of forgiveness did not surface for decades, because it is scary and ultimately leads to the big question: Who are we if we forgive and let go of our past? In the years that followed the murder attempt on my life, it was easy to let the frustration, anger, resentment, and pain become the glue that held me together. It became part of my identity, traits, beliefs, and values. On that day I experienced the metaphorical death of the girl and woman I would have become and I became someone else. If I had to assess my damages like Sarah, then I was owed the life I lost.

The years following the trauma and the trial were filled with heaviness and darkness. I was in a place where everything I knew came crashing down, a place where there was no hope, no light at the end of the tunnel, no sense to the madness, no justice to the injustice. I felt alone, isolated, and unsure of my place in the world, and I could not remember where I belonged. I tried to make sense of what was happening, and I questioned why a loving God would let me go through something so vile, unsettling, devastating, heartbreaking, and soul crushing.

The first time I started to experience anger was during my private hospital stay. As I was lying in the bed, a nurse came to check on me, take my vitals, and write in my chart. She offered some compassion and understanding by telling me about someone close to her who had experienced the same trauma. She recalled how devastating it was for her family, but, she said, in time it was possible to get through it and heal. This was a kind act, but I felt so conflicted. I wanted to scream, "Get out, I don't want to hear your story," and at the same time I wanted to say, "Hold me, I am so scared." Once again, I was presented with a choice. I chose not to accept the compassion and understanding from the nurse, but instead to hold onto the anger. The anger I had was directed at the wrong person, because deep down I was angry at the person who did this to me and I was not willing to forgive. Most people avoid forgiveness like the plague because we do not want to look at our own shortcomings, our own wounds.

While holding on to this need to not forgive, I subconsciously started to succumb to negative emotions. I succumbed to fear because it was easier than surrendering to courage. Fear brought me comfort, and it kept me shackled to this new reality and navigating life from a place of dread. It was a disconnected place that did not allow for meaningful engagement. In this place, I could create whatever I wanted without the responsibility of embracing true purpose. I could be the creator of a pretend life from this place of fear instead of embracing courage and living an authentic life.

I succumbed to resentment because it was easier than surrendering to forgiveness. Carrying deep-seated resentment for the darkness I had to bear brought me comfort, and every decision I made came from a place of resentment. I felt resentment toward God, the perpetrators, the wrongdoers, life, possibilities, and opportunities. Everything became outwardly focused because it was easier to blame, punish, accuse, condemn, hate, begrudge, and harbor bitter indignation at the unfairness of it all. I held onto the inability to forgive as I allowed resentment to fester unchecked.

I succumbed to self-pity because it was easier than surrendering to self-compassion. I became so involved in my problems I did not even realize others existed and had their own problems. The self-pity allowed me to abandon any interconnection with anyone else, and it allowed me to feel as if I were the only one in this world who was suffering. After all, I felt like I had been given the right to feel this way. I looked at everyone else going about their day as if nothing happened, undisturbed, and as I despised their flawless lives, I fell deeper into self-pity. I watched in slow motion as the world was moving ahead at a rapid pace without anyone noticing my pain.

I succumbed to anger because it was easier than surrendering to peace. Without realizing it, I became accustomed to being angry. I was mad because I felt powerless, violated, mistreated, disrespected, hurt, and taken advantage of, and I grieved parts of me that were dead. There is a saying that "an eye for an eye makes the whole world blind," but I did not care. I wanted an eye for an eye, justice, pain, and misery. I am always told, "Treat people the way you wish to be treated," but I could not see the logic in that because it only made sense to treat people well if they treated me well. In my life, I succumbed to anger in many situations, the injustice of not getting a raise at work, the job I wanted, the diagnosis I could have done without, or the endless cheating lessons I did not need to learn. In my angry moments, I wanted everyone to understand my wounds, sadness, and hurt and to lend me the understanding by agreeing with my anger and thoughts of vengeance. I am thankful to my intuition for not allowing me to act on my anger, believing it was justified. Nothing good could have come from acting on my anger.

There came the point in my life when my way of life no longer served me. It was a point when fear, resentment, self-pity, and anger only brought more darkness. Through holding onto these emotions and not forgiving, I opened myself up to attract life experiences that brought similar negative emotions like guilt, shame, anxiety, loneliness, embarrassment, humiliation, regret, doubt, and dissatisfaction. The burden of carrying all this darkness became too heavy a cross to bear, and it was slowly taking a toll on my health. Yet, despite this all-consuming heaviness, I was once again brought to a place of stillness.

I realized I allowed the villains to control my life by holding onto the monsters and not accepting things the way they were. If I was going to live life for me and experience life as intended, it was up to me to make a choice. I was tired of carrying the burdens of my past, and I wanted to live my life untethered to the things that were holding me back. I wondered if, just like Sarah, I had a steel hook in my side with a tether to my past and somehow I was keeping this villain alive while sacrificing my life. Decades had passed, and I was still dragging that part of my dark past along with me all the while resisting forgiveness. Like Sarah, I wondered when the right time was to forgive.

During a period of self-reflection following a cancer diagnosis that brought me full circle, to the point in which I once again came face to face with my mortality, I realized the only way to live a life of joy and inner peace was to let go of the past and forgive. I also could not help but wonder to what extent holding onto the past contributed to the disease. This realization brought up another challenge for me. If resisting forgiveness and holding onto negative emotions was the glue that held me together and informed the way I engaged with life, then who would I be without it, and would I be a healthier version of myself?

This question led me on a quest of self-discovery. It all started with a discussion with a close family member and spiritual guru, Darshana Rama. She held space for me and encouraged me to be open to new beginnings and embrace the healing journey. While we were having one of our deep discussions about life and healing, Darshana gave me a link to a self-love workshop facilitated by a close friend of ours. I took the opportunity to explore and dive deep into the world of self-love and self-discovery, which would ultimately change the course of my life.

At the workshop, we dealt with several aspects of self-development, but the topic that resonated with me was forgiveness. As the facilitator ran through the forgiveness checklist that included, "I don't have to forgive anyone," "They did not apologize to me," "They ruined my life," and so on, one in particular stood out for me: "My resentment keeps me safe."

That was my aha moment. I learned there that forgiveness opens our hearts to self-love. My self-righteous behavior created my prison, my small cell with just a glimpse of light. I knew holding onto the pain and not forgiving was like swallowing a teaspoon of poison every day, waiting for the other person to feel the effects. In truth, by not being willing to forgive, I was only hurting myself. I did not love myself enough to forgive and set myself free. The "they" or "the villain" did not even care or were even aware, but I kept on hurting myself by refusing to let go of the past. At that point, the facilitator asked us to join a forgiveness ritual, and I was happy to partake in because I felt ready to meet the new version of myself: the one who was no longer defined by her past but the one who sets herself free.

The heaviness, stress, and anxiety that clouded my life was my creation, and I wanted out. I no longer wanted to sleepwalk through my life or merely exist. I wanted to feel life the way it was intended. I wanted to live and experience the wonders that life had to offer, and I wanted to be free. In choosing to forgive, I had to see the villains in my life as people who had their own lives filled with their own experiences, good or bad. Just like Sarah accepted her villain, the boy who killed her mother and brother, as a person, I had to come to a place of acceptance. I remembered that Gabor Maté in his book *When the Body Says No*, described acceptance as the willingness to recognize and accept how things are. It is the courage to permit negative thinking to inform our understanding without allowing it to define our approach to the future. Acceptance does not demand becoming resigned to the continuation of whatever circumstances may trouble us, but it does require a refusal to deny exactly how things happen to be now. It challenges the deeply held belief that we are not worthy enough or "good" enough to be whole. Acceptance implies a compassionate relationship with oneself. It means discarding the double standard that, as we have seen, too often characterizes our relationship with the world. I wanted to find this courage to not let my past define my future; I wanted to feel joy and peace in life the way it was, not what I wished it would have been. I wanted to feel worthy enough to be whole and live a joyful life.

Throughout the ritual, I wondered if I was worthy of this act of self-love and self-compassion called forgiveness. I sat down and I wrote two letters: one for myself and one to all the villains in my life. In these letters, I expressed acceptance for the incidents that were done, I chose to see the villains as people, I practiced self-compassion and showed compassion for others, and I forgave myself for my choices. I accepted life for how things were, and I gave myself permission to be okay with it. Later that day, during a fire ceremony, I burned the letters, and as I watched them perish in the fire, I could feel the dark prison walls of unforgiveness crumble. At that moment, I could feel the light.

The most important lesson following this ritual was the power to change was always within me. I was happy my journey of self-discovery showed me how to actively live my chosen life and make decisions that support my desire to live and not exist. I loved myself enough to make the choice to forgive from a place of understanding and compassion, releasing the hold of my past traumatic experiences. In setting myself free, I released the fear of freedom that frightened me for so long, and in doing so my mental and physical health improved and I gained closure. Forgiveness was the best gift I gave myself.

CHAPTER SEVEN:

COURAGE AND SURRENDER

"Our deepest wounds surround our greatest gifts."
—KEN PAGE

Stacey Kramer told a story of a beautifully wrapped gift she was presented with, but before it could be opened, she shared some incredible things such a gift would do for you. This gift would bring the family together. It would make you feel loved and appreciated like never before and reconnected to friends and acquaintances you hadn't heard from in years. Adoration and admiration would overwhelm you. It would recalibrate what's most important in your life. It would redefine your sense of spirituality and faith, and you'd have a new understanding and trust in your body. You'd have unsurpassed vitality and energy, you'd expand your vocabulary, meet new people, and have a healthier lifestyle. As a bonus, you'd have an eight-week vacation of doing absolutely nothing. You would eat countless gourmet meals; flowers would arrive by the truckload. People would tell you you looked great and ask if you had any work done, and you'll have a lifetime supply of good drugs. You'd be challenged, inspired, motivated, and humbled. Your life would have new meaning, peace, health, serenity, happiness, and nirvana.

This unique gift came to her in what she describes as a rare gem: a brain tumor. This gift was not what she would wish on anyone, but she acknowledged it profoundly altered her life in ways she didn't expect. Her message was the next time you're faced with something unexpected, unwanted, and uncertain, consider it just may be a gift.

Listening to Stacey, I remembered my cancer diagnosis and wondered if the cancer was a gift, and if it was, what it brought me. A few months earlier, I found myself sitting in silence on a bench in the hospital with my best friend, silenced by the words I heard in a consultation room just one floor down: You have cancer. Let me rewind. It was a joyful time, and I was at a beautiful lunch. My friend told me she was expecting a baby, a miracle baby. She and her husband had been trying to conceive for years, and finally God had blessed them with this miracle. We were so excited, and over the months that followed, we planned for the baby's arrival. Pregnancy complications landed my friend in the hospital, and I was with her as she navigated the uncertainty facing her and her unborn baby. Seven months into the pregnancy, my friend and her loving husband welcomed their second child prematurely.

While my friend adjusted to life as a mommy to a premature baby, I embarked on an unknown venture of my own, a biopsy. On a routine check, doctors discovered a lump that presented as distorted tissue. This raised some concern and suspicion as to its nature, which prompted further investigation, hence the biopsy. The procedure was pretty painless, and I remained optimistic about the outcome. In fact, my thoughts were positive. The following Friday, I had an appointment with my surgeon to receive the results from the biopsy. Before the appointment, I spent some time with my best friend celebrating her baby who by then was a week old. I excused myself to pop downstairs for a quick consultation.

Downstairs in the consultation room, on Friday the thirteenth, my doctor explained how my life was about to change over the months that followed. She was reassuring and empathetic in her manner. She explained there would be a cancer treatment plan put in place that would direct the course of my treatment from a medical perspective. From an emotional perspective, she encouraged the support of family and friends over the months that lay ahead, and she asked me to return the following week for a further discussion. As I left the consultation room, I had to process what I had heard. I had cancer, and there was no way to run away from it, no way around it. The only way was through it. I now had to pop back upstairs to my friend, but I was unsure of what I was going to say. As the elevator doors opened, I could only manage to walk to the bench, and there I sat. Out of nowhere, someone sat down next to me. It was my best friend. She had been to visit her baby in the neonatal ward and found me sitting on a bench in the late afternoon in a deserted hallway. All I could muster to her inquiring about the consultation was, "Cancer, I have cancer." We sat together and held space for each other given the circumstances where we found ourselves at that point in our life. The next day I shared the news of the diagnosis with my loved ones. I knew this would be hard for them to hear, and it was, but the love and support I received was overwhelming.

The following week I was back for another consultation to discuss all the details I could not take in on the day of the diagnosis, including an immediate treatment plan. Over the next few months, I had to undergo two surgeries, radiotherapy, and endocrine treatment. My first surgery was on the night of the blood moon, and as I sat in my hospital bed, I remembered the meaning attributed to a blood moon was a new beginning. I wondered if cancer brought me a new beginning and if it was possible. Would I have the courage to embrace this new beginning? At the next consultation, I was told a second surgery was required, which I then had. After healing, I started radiotherapy as chemotherapy was not recommended to me as a treatment. Every radiotherapy session had me glued to the hospital. I did not realize it, but there is no time for making plans when you undergo cancer treatment. My life pretty much revolved around home, hospital, and treatments.

As Stacey mentioned in her talk, I experienced the profound gift the cancer diagnosis brought. Like Stacey, this cancer brought my family together; I felt loved and appreciated like never before, and I reconnected with friends and acquaintances. I had a new sense of what was most important in my life. It redefined my sense of spirituality and faith by seeking meaning and purpose in this trauma. I had a new understanding and trust in my body, because I realized as I was undergoing treatment my body knew what to do to protect my organs from the radiation. If that meant I retained water and became bigger, then I was in awe of its intelligence. I had unsurpassed vitality and energy because I had to make a conscious choice to reduce my stress and focus on practices that supported a peaceful existence.

After all the treatments were complete, it felt like I was at the beginning of life, like a twenty-year-old deciding where to go from here. Coming face to face with my mortality once more allowed for self-examination and reassessment of my life, continued existence, and purpose. I looked at the spiritual motivations behind the disease, which was that God needed me to pay attention to my life and engage with it in a meaningful way. The cancer journey came to me at a point in my life where I desperately needed to engage with my life in a more meaningful way. Until that point, I was leading a full life, but one that was empty and lonely. In many ways, I am grateful because the experience brought me the courage to transform, and I learned that these situations, as bad as they may seem, can happen for us and protect us in ways we don't even know.

This meant my most enriching experiences were not found in superficial pleasures, but in my most painful sorrow and despair.

When I used to go to the hospital, I was asked how I kept such a good, positive outlook with everything. The reality was sadness, distress, depression, fear, and anxiety were all normal feelings I experienced when I learned about cancer, but at the same time, it was important for me to accept and feel every emotion in the moment. I allowed myself to lean into the discomfort that comes with feeling emotions and respond in a way that supported healthy processing and healing. Having good self-awareness, I knew talking about the cancer was the better option because it helped me cope, and it also helped my loved ones understand what I was going through, and it also gave them an indication of how they should treat me. In addition, I continued to meet with my psychologist to work through some of the core emotions and feelings associated with going through the process. At the later stages of healing, I attended support groups to share my cancer journey that helped process the experience by talking about it, and there I learned the value of interconnected healing by exchanging stories with survivors.

As a spiritual being, I knew what was happening to me was much bigger than me, giving me the courage and freedom to trust in God. I knew God would not forsake me, and his angels and everyone from the spirit world would be with me through every step I took. Seeing a bigger meaning for the cancer diagnosis helped me maintain a positive mindset irrespective of what lay ahead. With this attitude, I could go to every doctor's appointment and treatment with a smile on my face, knowing I was not alone. I had my loved ones here in the physical world and the spiritual world going with me, and it made all the difference.

Years before my cancer diagnosis, following the murder attempt on my life, I was given advice I did not understand. I was told to "hand my sorrow over and lay my troubles at God's feet." I was told I could not win this battle by myself and if I asked for help, I would receive it. As I was navigating my cancer journey, the advice made sense for the first time in my life, and I instinctively knew how to do this. I understood that everything that happened to me brought me an opportunity to choose. It became easier to surrender to God's plan because I understood my life had value in this almighty cosmos. My life was as important as the sun in the sky, or the earthworm working tirelessly somewhere underground. My life was important enough for God to pay attention to me.

The realization made me weep, and it led to a memory of the time I spent in the Rocky Mountains in Canada. The trip held beautiful memories for me of having spent quality time with family. Still, most of all, I remembered how much perspective I gained from standing next to the lake, gazing out over the beautiful mountains. The mountains were majestic, covered in lush greenery, and the lake seemed vast and endless. The sheer size of the mountain range, the clear waters of the lake, and the ice caps were breathtaking. It was Mother Nature at her best. I could feel the chill in the air on my skin, and I realized how insignificant I was by comparison to God's creations, and taking it all in was so incredibly overwhelming. Yet, at that moment, I found respect for the land and my place in this universe.

During my cancer journey, I talked to God often and said, "I know you have walked the path ahead of me, and you have seen what I cannot see. As I walk through the valley of the shadow of death, I will not fear. I ask that you wash me in your blood, and today I lay all my troubles at your feet, and in You, I will trust." Still, no matter how well I felt or could cope with my diagnosis, as a human, I was tested. These experiences have a way of bringing you to your knees, literally and figuratively.

My surrender experience began the moment I was willing to release the outcome of my diagnosis and allow a Higher Power to guide me. It started when I stopped making my plans and plotting strategies of what I thought my life should be but instead woke up to the realization that we don't make plans; God does. I started to access the magnificence of living in the present moment in a new and fresh way. When I began to change the way I was doing and saying things and living from a place where I no longer aimed to control the future, I started to experience each moment directly, as it is. I began to live life in color, and through my journey, I discovered surprise and mystery. This newfound awakening through surrender helped me to get through the cancer journey.

That feeling brought me to a place of humility that allowed me to lean into my surrender experience through six steps. I started to surrender through prayer. I started to submit my desires and fears to God through prayer, allowing the Holy Spirit to guide and wait for Him to answer. My prayers became purposeful, faithful, forever conscious of the loving presence of God. Through prayer, I experienced faith that allowed me the courage to continue beyond what the eye can see.

I remembered to breathe the breath of God. It is the first thing we do when we come into this world and the last thing we do when we leave it. In the morning and evening, I would sit on my bed and do a breathing exercise. I would close my eyes and focus on what I felt around me and within. I would take note of the sensations in my body, connect, and if I felt the presence of emotions, I would allow them to be there. I would not hold onto thoughts and release them as they come and go. I remembered at that moment I did not have to be anywhere or do anything. I would notice the movement in my body with each breath and allow my body to relax into breathing in no particular rhythm. This would continue for about twelve to fifteen minutes. More than that, I breathed the breath of God that connected me to the world beyond what the physical eye can see.

I surrendered and awakened to the true value of time. When coming face to face with my mortality, yet again, I realized just how precious time was. If you do not spend time wisely, it will slip through your fingers. I live my life as if every day is my last, because when the angel of death appears and says, "It's time to go," I want to be ready instead of trying to reschedule and renegotiate. I want the peace of knowing I lived a life of purpose and meaning, and at the point of final departure, there was no unfinished business.

I started to be more intentional with the things I desired in my life and the choices I had to make, and I also accepted that I am not alone. I have much support in the physical world, but I have equally as much support from the spirit world. Knowing that gives me the faith to trust and know I am guided by a force far greater than me. I started to be clear when I asked for guidance and pay attention as I waited to receive it. It has never steered me wrong. According to a *Healthline* article, a growing body of research suggests there's a strong connection between your mind and your body. It isn't yet understood how vibrational energy fits into the relationship between the two, but vibrational energy experts claim certain emotions and thought patterns, such as joy, peace, and acceptance, create high frequency vibrations, while other feelings and mindsets, such as anger, despair, and fear, vibrate at a lower rate. There isn't much scientific evidence to support this correlation, but there is plenty of evidence linking positive emotions and thinking patterns to better health. I found that throughout the surrender process, my frequency vibrations were higher, as through these practices I experienced joy and peace and living courageously.

I surrendered through gratitude, which is the most creative force in the universe. Gratitude helped me to see what was there instead of what wasn't. Before I could even experience gratitude, I had to be grateful for who I was, what I had, and who I was about to become. So I started to thank God every day for providing unique gifts into my life, and this was evidence enough for me to realize the abundance and blessings I already have each day. I started focusing on the good in my life, and I began to count my blessings. I wake up and am thankful for the weather, rain or sunshine, the sound of the birds, my dog that jumps on my bed with muddy paws, and family and friends who drop by unannounced. Once I experienced gratitude, I started seeing the beauty in everything; the things that annoyed me became precious.

These were my six steps to surrender on my inward spiritual journey. I realized I could not control what was already in the making. I could only navigate what was given to me as part of a bigger plan and accept what was happening to me. I chose to accept my path graciously, practice self-love and self-compassion, and that gave me inner peace. The cancer was not controlling my response to life. I was not my cancer, my cancer was a mere visitor, and together we navigated my body and my life until this visitor called cancer had to leave.

While my spiritual surrender was an inward journey, I also had some outward aids that worked while recuperating. For example, lying in bed, I read so many inspirational books, and I came across this quote in *Inner Engineering: A Yogi's Guide to Joy* that resonated with my surrender experience beautifully. Sadhguru says, "Believing means you have assumed something that you do not know; seeking means you have realized that you do not know." I also listened to inspirational music that brought revelation and hope. I took the time to do something for myself that nobody could take away from me, so I listened to educational DVDs and learned a new language. I absorbed the unconditional love I received from my pets, and when I had the energy, I took short walks in nature.

I chose to embrace my surrender experience by creating ways to enhance the cancer diagnosis and journey that followed after it happened to me. Still, we don't all need to be brought to a complete halt, onto our knees literally and figuratively, or experience a traumatic life event like a dreaded disease. Instead, we can encourage our surrender experience arrival through daily practice on a small scale in the moments that are okay. This will only help and prepare us for those times when even the idea of practicing surrender will be untenable.

To practice, we surrender to what is right now. We drop into our direct experience, what we are sensing, feeling, living in this moment. We agree to feel life, as it is now, without our mind adding, taking away, manipulating, or doing anything whatever to it. Surrender, at its core, is the willingness to meet life as it is, to stop fighting with or trying to change what is so, right now. And remarkably, no matter the catalyst, or whether it is a moment's surrender or a lifetime's, the result or gift that accompanies it remains the same: acceptance, gratitude, grace, inner peace, and joy.

Surrender is a state of being, something that, with awareness, we can invite into our lives. And thankfully, when we have no other choice but to surrender the illusion of control, we can experience the profundity and aliveness of this present moment and the gift of it. We can experience the presence of something larger and unknowable; we can experience ourselves being guided down the current that is life, the current we are part of. Then, having tasted surrender, we can relax and trust—and know it's safe to let go and live courageously. Just like Stacey, my unexpected, unwanted, and uncertain encounter with cancer brought me the gift of courage and surrender.

CHAPTER EIGHT:

THE VAGINA KEEPS THE SCORE

―――

"Everything in the world is about sex except sex. Sex is about power."

—OSCAR WILDE

Robynette, a young Indian girl, was only three years old when her stepfather invited her to play a game with him. She remembered this game being fun as they sat behind the magazine pages filled with pictures of different shapes, sizes, colors, and sparkles. She recalls her stepdad asking her to point out what her favorite ones were on the page. She pointed and said, "I like the pink one, I want the sparkly one." This magazine was a sex paraphernalia catalog, and little Robynette was invited to choose her preferred sex toy. That was how the grooming started.

Robynette described the relationship with her stepfather as special at the time; they were very close and did everything together. She recalls family and friends commenting on how beautiful their relationship was, father and daughter. To the outside world, everything seemed normal, but behind closed doors, she was being groomed as a sexual partner.

The first sexual acts started with participating in touching genitals. She recalled him coming into her room that she shared with her sister, crawling into bed with her, and molesting her. To anyone at home, it seemed like she was being tucked in for the night, but they were having their special time. This was normal to Robynette because these were the only memories she had, and she did not know anything else. This was the kind of things that you and your stepdad do, she thought.

To keep her silence, he would buy her gifts, and she recalls feeling special. As always, he would tell her, "We don't talk about the things that we do, because it is special." Robynette said the sexual abuse was not only when she was awake. There were many nights when she would wake up with her stepfather in her bed on top of her having sex with her. The abuse went on for years without Robynette realizing it was abuse.

One afternoon after school, Robynette invited her ten-year-old friend over to play. She described her stepfather entering the room and touching her friend's legs inappropriately. He then rubbed lotion on her legs and left the room. At that point, her friend told her she was very uncomfortable and her dad never did that to her and nobody should touch your body inappropriately.

At this point, I enquired whether Robynette felt jealous as this was her special activity with her dad. She said no, but in that moment, she recalled walking in on her parents having sex in their bedroom. She knew what they were doing, and she recalled feeling angry, slamming the door, and storming downstairs. In that moment, she said, "I never knew why I reacted and felt that way, but today I realized that I was jealous because that was what we did during our special time."

At age twelve, her stepfather was called away to work in a different city. Robynette recalled her mom having a talk with her and her sister following a telephone call about her stepfather. The call was from his son from another marriage, informing them he had molested his five-year-old daughter, the stepfather's granddaughter. Robynette's mom was concerned and enquired if he ever touched them inappropriately. Robynette's sister replied with a firm no, but Robynette could not find the words, and her tears spoke when she could not.

She was so scared because she was worried what her mom would say and think about her, not realizing she wasn't in the wrong at all. She was just a child. Her mother asked Robynette, "Did he have sex with you?" She replied with a low "yes." Her mother asked the same of her sister, she said no. According to Robynette, that was the last time her mother ever spoke to her about it.

As a result of her mother and sister never speaking about the abuse, Robynette was further traumatized because she never got the help she needed. She was left to doubt whether her mom believed her at all. She described her mother as a proud person who was easily embarrassed but recognizes she may have been hurt by this situation happening under her nose and carried the shame associated with the situation.

Robynette recalled her mom telling them when they suffered financial difficulties that they were not to let family or the outside world know about their challenges but to pretend that everything was fine. Robynette's sexual abuse was handled the same way, swept under the carpet to never be spoken about again.

Robynette is of the view that in traditional Indian society, sexual abuse is heavily stigmatized by shame. According to the September 2020 research paper "Child Sexual Abuse: A Stigma for Society":

Abuse is defined as any action that intentionally harms or injures another person. Many people assume, abuse means physical violence, that's not always the case. Abuse can come in many forms, such as: physical or verbal maltreatment, injury, assault, violation, rape, unjust practices, crimes, other types of aggression etc. Children are a vulnerable part of our society and presently child sexual abuse has become a great concern around the world. Such cases against children are reported from all spheres like home, school as well as in their neighborhood. The majority of children and teens are most likely to be sexually abused by someone they know and trust such as their own family members, neighbors and staff at their school.

If we turn to the world figure on child sexual abuse, we know from the Violence Against Children page on the WHO website that in the year 2002, the World Health Organization estimated seventy-three million boys and 150 million girls under the age of eighteen years had experienced various forms of sexual violence. A meta-analysis conducted in the year 2009 analyzed sixty-five studies covering twenty-two countries reflected that the highest prevalence rate of child sexual abuse was seen in Africa, at 34.4 percent. More recently, on June 8, 2020, the World Health Organization found that globally, up to one billion children aged two to seventeen years have experienced physical, sexual, or emotional violence or neglect in the past year. This is a substantial increase and reflects the seriousness and vastness of the problem.

Sexual violence has a lifelong impact on our health and sexual well-being. According to the World Health Organization, children exposed to violence and other adversities can result in negative coping and health risk behaviors and are substantially more likely to smoke, misuse alcohol and drugs, and engage in high-risk sexual behavior. They also have higher rates of anxiety, depression, other mental health problems, and suicide.

Robynette shared with me that from a young age she had an unhealthy obsession with sex. During the time of her trauma, she was exposed to pornography, and that created a silent addiction that as a child she didn't understand. She started masturbating and watching porn at a young age. After an ordinary family movie night, she would wake up early the next morning to rewind the movie to rewatch the sex scenes. Later in high school, she became more adventurous and took nude pictures for distribution to anyone interested.

She was under the misimpression that all guys wanted was sex, even though as a tween she didn't understand what sex was about—only what she was exposed to during her abuse. This led to her being sexually active at a very young age, unprotected with an older man. Robynette recalls disrespecting herself and allowing other to do the same. She told me she became flirtatious and participated in risky sexual behavior. For a long time Robynette believed she was unworthy of true love and a healthy sexual relationship.

According to the "Changes in Women's Sexual Behavior Following Sexual Assault" research paper, some researchers have suggested, "Women may exhibit an increase in sexual activity post-assault. Such outcomes are not mutually exclusive possibilities but may instead reflect subtypes of sexual assault victims. A significant percentage of assault survivors did report increases in sexual activity following trauma."

An increase in sexual activity was my experience following my rape and attempted murder. It started innocently, with one sexual partner, my boyfriend at the time whom I felt I could be in control with during our sexual encounters. Soon, it was not enough to satisfy my deep need for control. I started looking for control everywhere, and there was no status off-limits, single, taken, married, old, young, Black, White, Asian—it was all fair game. I remember going out with friends for a night on the town. While my friends were enjoying themselves, I scouted for a potential sexual partner and possibly another lined up for later. Having more than one sexual partner was not unusual, and at the time I did not understand this behavior; all I knew was I needed to be in charge.

This behavior carried on for a long time, until one day, I visited my gynecologist, and my vagina was no longer a willing participant and refused to open. My vagina had shut down, and I could not lay blame. I learned that the muscles in my vagina had sealed shut. My PTSD that was in my body was also in my vagina, and it was called vaginismus.

When we experience trauma, our bodies remember and react in a certain way. Following the attempt on my life, I felt unsafe in my home. This meant that every time I came home, I had to show my body it was safe to be home alone and that no one was there to attack me. This meant I had to retrain my body to know that being at home alone was safe. The same was the case for my vagina, and this led me to work with a sexologist and psychologist to help me understand my behavior and retrain my body and become comfortable with my sexuality to have a healthy sex life.

The book *The Body Keeps the Score*, by Bessel van der Kolk, stated trauma victims cannot recover until they become familiar with and befriend the sensations of their bodies. Being frightened means you live in a body that is always on guard. So, I was living in a body that was always on guard, including my vagina. The bodies of child abuse victims are tense and defensive until they find a way to relax and feel safe. This was true for Robynette too. In order to change, people need to become aware of their sensations and the way their bodies interact with the world around them. Physical self-awareness is the first step in releasing the tyranny of the past.

I was fortunate to catch up with Washington, DC, based certified trauma professional and sexual health coach Laura Zam. Laura is also a survivor of childhood sexual trauma. Growing up, she had a very loving family, but she also happened to live on a block shared by two pedophiles. According to Laura, these men molested scores of neighborhood children, including her. She was also sexually abused by a teenager around this time. She was four when most of this abuse occurred. Based on her experience, Laura is on a mission to help others reclaim sexual vitality as a way to reach their own potential.

During our meeting, I asked Laura whether the body-mind-soul connection is the starting point for someone who wants to pursue a journey of recovery after experiencing rape, sexual abuse, molestation, or sexual trauma. She paused to think for a second and told me she takes a slightly different approach to heal sexual trauma, and I loved what she had to say:

When we talk about the mind-body connection, at the core of healing is self-awareness, especially if we're going to include modalities like meditation, mindfulness, and yoga. When we bring these modalities in, it can get a little far away from sex, because it's about being present in the moment, and in the bedroom it is about being physical.

Healing modalities often do not include the lower body and don't include strategies for what to do when we are in the bedroom. Laura expressed delight at the fact I worked with a sexologist because it's a whole other experience and all of that can be useful, but it's incomplete. It's incomplete because when we are in the bedroom and someone has a sexual agenda, they're aroused, and they want something from us, and the reality is that we either have the skills to deal with that person's desire or we don't.

We also have our own desire, but because of our past experience, the abusive experience or upbringing, or a combination thereof, we may be attracted to some of this being right, not being there, or even being a little bit used. It is also possible at that moment to dissociate to have that control and to just say, "Well, I am just fucking this guy. I don't give a shit about him. Yeah, that was a good fuck." We see it as Laura explaining all these dynamics need a foundation of being present, but everything we do at that moment could very often just go out the window because what's going on in that moment has nothing to do with this.

Yes, it does fundamentally have to do with being present, except it's hard to access that zen presence, because what's going on in the bedroom is arousal and feeling blindsided by desire. Also, in those moments, it's about questioning what to do now that somebody is entering you, whether the penetration is easy or not, and at that point not knowing what to do. You don't know what to do with your vagina. Do you pull it away, open it up, or shut it down? The question is also if you can do it, because the vaginal muscles have a mind of their own. You cannot use your mind to think, "Vagina, open up," because it does not work. It will only open up when the body feels safe. For all these reasons, Laura starts sexual healing from a physical sexual place because that's what's going on in the bedroom.

Listening to Laura, I was transported to the sessions I had with my sexologist. The sessions were in the evening, and it always felt like time well spent. When I was in the first session, we explored my sexual history, my current sex life, my goals, and my intentions for what I wanted from the sessions.

We also spoke about what I remembered about sex growing up, my first experiences alone or with another person, my parents' attitudes, sex education or lack thereof, how I experienced puberty, what I was told about sex, what my feelings were about the menstrual cycle, whether I had any nonconsensual experiences or abuse, STD history, any gynecological conditions, pregnancy history, and more. Even though this sounds like a lot, I remember it not being an overwhelming conversation but merely a trip down memory lane.

In the later sessions, we explored my sexual partners, the question of whether I have in the past or was currently self-pleasuring, whether I was dating, whether there was or has been any infidelity, whether I had experienced an orgasm, how I felt about and whether I used sex toys, what worked and did not work for me, how I felt about initiating sex, my boundaries, whether I felt confident speaking up and communicating with my partner/s about sex, and what types of touch I responded to. There was also a physical component to the treatment that I was later introduced to.

Laura's starting point on the road to recovery were the four pillars of sexual healing in the bedroom. These need to be worked on first with oneself, and then if you have a partner you trust and have a loving relationship with, we can bring a partner into this healing. However, this trusting and loving relationship must be built on a foundation we establish ourselves.

In order to create this foundation, we establish first sexual safety, second sexual presence of being in our bodies in a sexual context with our own arousal. So, this goes beyond the mind-body connection because it deals with the physical aspect of sexual healing. We need to feel safe in the bedroom when we are experiencing arousal and we have all these other things like desire going on and we need to figure out if we can be present and respond physically from a place of safety.

The third aspect is pleasure and sexual pleasure education. Pleasure is the feeling of happy satisfaction and enjoyment, and pleasure education seeks to normalize the idea of giving and receiving pleasure, not only in sexual activity but in relationships. Pleasure education allows us to develop healthier relationships with ourselves and future partners, thereby increasing overall life satisfaction and happiness. Pleasure education has many ramifications; some of those are learning what we like and being able to communicate. In Laura's opinion, pleasure is an antidote to abuse, because abuse doesn't feel good and pleasure is like giving yourself doses of this antidote.

Over and over, anytime you give yourself sexual pleasure or any kind of indulgence, pleasure can have that function of being an antidote. Pleasure is like microdosing self-love by sending a message to yourself over and over when you give yourself any kind of gratification. "I deserve it. Pleasure is important, and I am important." Pleasure helps to rebalance ourselves, because following sexual trauma, we experience self-blame, self-doubt, and low self-esteem. So, it's important this form of self-love becomes a practice. The last thing pleasure does for us is it gives us the knowledge base we need to have an equitable sexual experience so we do not feel like someone's taking advantage of us, which is going to trigger us.

Sexual enjoyment formed part of my homework outside of the regular sessions. The instructions handed to me were clear. I had a diagram, a roadmap, to sexual pleasure. As I left the office with the piece of paper, I asked myself how badly I wanted to restore my sexual health, because there was this component that I have never explored. I knew that in society, touching myself in a sexual way is taboo. I was once again confronted with the decision to choose my sexual health over society or what anybody would think. This was a way for me to take my power back in the bedroom and empower myself. I did not want to be a victim in the bedroom, and I did not want this violent act to rob me of experiencing pleasurable intimacy.

That night and many days and nights after, I spent time with myself teaching my body sexual safety, sexual presence, and sexual pleasure. There was no way I could let anyone close unless I was able to feel safe in my body, present in my body, and comfortable with the experience of sexual pleasure. I needed to feel relaxed with myself to invite someone else to join. This practice helped me retrain my body to let go of fear and accept pleasure.

The final pillar to sexual healing, Laura explained, was sexual power. She said sexual power is tricky for survivors when we're not talking in a sex-specific context about healing. She said we miss this sexual power in the context of sexual healing on our recovery journey because it can become political, meaning there is a need for equality. However, in the bedroom, it's more complicated than women just having as many rights as the partner. Some of us go about searching for power, and we do not necessarily do it in the healthiest of ways. As a survivor of sexual trauma, Laura described her promiscuous behavior that included risky sexual behavior with multiple partners.

Reflecting on what Robynette told me, her promiscuous behavior included taking nude images and distributing them to those who requested them as well as risky sexual behavior with multiple partners. My promiscuous behavior was a direct consequence of PTSD, and it included risky sexual behavior with multiple partners to satisfy the hunger for control and power.

This showed me that no matter the sexual traumatic experience, we all face similar consequences. My saving grace was my sexologist confirmed I was not alone in my dilemma and there was nothing wrong with me. This was also confirmed by "Changes in Women's Sexual Behavior Following Sexual Assault," in which a significant percentage of assault survivors did report increases in sexual activity following trauma. This was what all of us experienced. Through our promiscuous behavior, we found community years later. Laura told me she does not pathologize her experiences, neither do Robynette nor I. Robynette looked back fondly without judgment and I thanked my experiences for what they brought to my life, and I am grateful I never contracted a disease and didn't get hurt.

According to Laura, finding sexual power is tricky, because the promiscuous behavior could present as power. It could feel like we have power; of course, it's not real, but it can taste like power. When it comes to sexual power, somebody has a sexual agenda, and that leads into the question, "What is my sexual agenda?" It could be that my sexual agenda is to set a boundary. My sexual agenda may be to say no, I don't want that, or I want to give permission in the moment. It could also be, "I don't want to have sex right now. I don't want to feel like somebody overpowering me and taking advantage of me." The tricky part about this is navigating competing agendas in the bedroom.

So, finding this very tricky power balance in the bedroom comes down to reclaiming our voice. The four pillars are not separate, but they all work together in knowing what a person likes sexually. And having the ability to talk about that, to negotiate that with a partner, allows for you to have a voice and be heard. Power is being able to feel you are able to pivot from activities or things that are happening in the bedroom in the moment that you don't like or feel triggering. So it's about coming into a sexual situation as a partner with knowledge and agency to act upon on a moment-to-moment basis.

Laura suggests there are two aspects to our sexuality. It starts with feeling safe to express our sexuality and being okay with someone looking at you and finding you attractive. Feeling sexy is a safety issue, because it takes a lot of safety and often a lot of work not to feel traumatized by the attention. It's about getting to a place where you can feel sexy and attractive and be okay with someone else finding you sexy and attractive. When we get here, we move beyond receiving someone's sexual interest, and there we find our own voice. Here, again, we step out of trauma and into our sexuality.

Another aspect of coming into our sexuality is where we can make requests. We can make requests and we can pivot in the moment so our pleasure is primary. We are an equal pleasure partner unless we are making a very specific agreement with someone, for example, "I'm tired. I'm just going to please you tonight, honey. It's okay." That way, my partner receives pleasure and is happy, and I'm going to enjoy it but I'll also get to go to sleep at a decent time. We should all have this position of power to make requests. If the other party is making demands, it could result in you not having a voice. Coming into our sexuality, according to Laura, is the four pillars coming together, but primarily, it's about this safety, being able to feel and receive someone's sexual interest, and expressing our own sexual interest while negotiating between the two.

Many survivors don't have skills training in developing this sense of power, and so we're just left to our own devices. We let people, even our loving partners, make love to us in a way that feels violating, and it's not that they're doing anything wrong. It's just we don't have a voice, so we feel like we are being violated or maybe we feel like we have power over them exclusively. The power, in that case, and the dissociation fit closely together because you are not necessarily present. In those moments, you become your own kind of fuck machine. In order not to slip into that state of mind, we must focus on finding our voice, being heard, and stepping out of trauma into your sexuality.

For other trauma survivors who have particular proclivities, such as BDSM with a desire to be, for example, tied down, there are options. Impact play is another way in which to safely have pain inflicted on the body. If someone has that physical sexual desire, there are whole communities that support people in figuring out ways to do that in a safe way. Laura says some therapists who aren't trained in sexuality may be of the opinion that participating in BDSM may be replaying your trauma. However, it's inherently retraumatizing, but it's not if a person has a structure and they have guidance to work with those healing elements.

Sexual healing has been liberating for me, and it all started with a decision to participate in my healing and taking the action required. This part of my journey was about taking my sexual power back. What I have learned is we all suffer differently, but it has the hallmarks that could be the same. In our quiet moments and in a community, we heal, and it starts with the courage to choose and take action. Healing sexually was one of the best gifts I ever gave myself to step out of sexual trauma into sexual safety, pleasure, presence, and power.

CHAPTER NINE:

LIVING AUTHENTICALLY

―

"The privilege of a lifetime is to become who you truly are."
—CARL JUNG

In today's life, despite many accomplishments, supposed happiness, friendships, and wealth, many people feel a sense of emptiness, lack of fulfillment, and discomfort from within. This is because many of us are subconsciously or consciously seeking to live an authentic life. The satisfaction that nothing from the outside world can fulfill. Reaching to live an authentic life seems easy enough when we say the words, but examining it closely can be scary when we have to face ourselves.

In our society, we are conditioned to look to the outside world for the missing pieces to fill that void when we seek to live an authentic life. We are constantly exposed to so much content through various media campaigns and social media, and we succumb and end up buying things we don't want. We take pictures to fill our Instagram feed, reflecting the beautiful lives we live. We are constantly encouraged to associate success with clothing, makeup, lifestyle, yachts, champagne, and luxury. In the end, it all steers to serve as validation of who we are temporarily, but true authentic living is not a byproduct of this façade.

When we are forced to face ourselves through life's challenges like economic pressures, loss of finances, loss of a home, death of a loved one, a diagnosis, failed relationships, divorce, tragedy, debt, or the inability to achieve, we find ourselves at an uncertain place where we have to reflect and be content with the person we are. Most people are afraid of looking at themselves and recognizing the person they are or who they have become. Unfortunately, most people choose to numb the pain with alcohol, drugs, risky behavior, or avoiding matters by throwing themselves into their work in an attempt to escape the discomfort and the feeling of being lost.

For others, these challenges bring about questions like, "Who am I?" "Am I living a life that is true to who I am at my core?" For those people, the meaning and purpose of life become essential, and they seek the quest to live a meaningful life that is authentic. Reaching this place of awareness is a pivotal point in one's life because we start to let go of who we are to embrace the new version of ourselves, the authentic person who accepts all parts.

Dr. Maria Sirois in her TEDx talk says that Jalāl al-Dīn Rumi wrote that you have a duty to perform. Do anything else, do any number of things, occupy your time fully, and yet, if you do not do this task, all your time will have been wasted. What he is telling us is it is up to us to come alive, fully alive, in the one life that we can live and move away from the limitations that keep us confined. He was telling us to step into the unique particular being that we are, each one of us.

This is by no means an easy task. I recall my deep sorrow following the attack on my life, how I mourned the loss of the girl who died metaphorically: the life I lost, the person who I was supposed to be who now would never exist. Grief has a way of distorting how we perceive things, and I could not see the life that awaited because I was fixated on the one I lost. Instead of embracing my unique self and accepting life in the moment, I subconsciously decided to create the life I thought I was owed. Over the years that followed, I created a holistic life: physical health (check), family (check), relationships (check), career (check), wealth and money (check), and religion and spiritual wellness (check).

There was one problem: I felt like an impostor, like I was living someone else's life.

In her TED talk, "Listening to Shame," Brené Brown explained that one thing we can do is reframe vulnerability as a brave act. She pointed out people often don't show vulnerability because they don't want to seem weak. But when we do open up, others are more likely to applaud our bravery than to judge us. In other words, one way we can work to be more authentic is by reminding ourselves that being vulnerable and authentic is actually a sign of bravery and courage. This was a hard step to take because I had to accept my vulnerability and admit to myself I was not living an authentic life. It came down to making a choice to live an authentic life. That meant evaluating how I was experiencing my life and whether that experience served me well. I found it didn't serve me, and only I had the power to change it. It was one of the hardest but most courageous and liberating discoveries I have made. I accepted my choices and experiences, and I allowed myself to be proud of the life I built. The truth was I was flourishing living "someone else's" life until I wasn't. It became more important than ever for me to live my authentic life and become the person I was always meant to be.

As mentioned before, life circumstances have a way of presenting us with unimaginable challenges, and when these come around, it requires quiet reflection. It needs us to look at our lives and evaluate who we are, who we want to be, and what we want to achieve. Living an inauthentic life served up some serious challenges for me: loss of a job, loss of a relationship, loss of a home, financial pressures, disease, stress, anxiety, loss of sleep, constant racing thoughts, and all negativity associated with this happening simultaneously. Trying to hide behind a mask when your life falls apart is a real thing. I desperately wanted to keep up the illusion of a well-put-together life, but I found that in doing so, joy, inner peace, and authenticity could not be achieved. At this juncture of my life where I was given an opportunity to step out of a life of façade and into an authentic life, I was once again presented with a choice to rebel, live behind a mask, succumb to negative emotions, remain in a hopeless situation, or choose to change my perspective and see how all these things happening to me were happening for me.

With this new perspective, I chose myself and actively decided to change my situation, as hard as it was. During this time of my life, I learned holding onto the past will suck the joy out of the present. I could not allow my past to ruin my present, so with great difficulty, I made the choice to let go. I was craving freedom, joy, inner peace, and authenticity, and I was the only person who could give it to myself. The experience of letting go felt like a metamorphosis, a shedding of a past life that became meaningless. This reminded me of my surrender experience, another transformation that fundamentally changed my state of self and direction of my life.

When we step into our authentic lives, we become the authors of our lives. We have our own ideas, our own way of being, our unique way of doing. When we operate our life from this place of vulnerability, we are empowered because we cancel out the noise from everyone else, and we stay true to our core values, beliefs, and intuition. Just like my surrender experience, this metamorphosis started with relinquishing that which no longer served me.

I relinquished ignorance and welcomed awareness. Creating a healthy awareness in my life started with the willingness to want to change. Starting with my thoughts, I learned to be aware of my thought patterns and self-talk. I had to sift through the negative thoughts and limiting beliefs that I had been telling myself or originated from what others told me. I remember having this limiting belief from a partner telling me all I had were pipe dreams. I believed that for the longest time, but when I became aware of the limiting belief, I changed it by thinking differently through the help of therapy and self-love coaching. I now believe I can make my dreams come true, and every day I am pleasantly surprised by how this has become my reality. Over time, working with my psychologist and self-love coach, I rooted out most negative beliefs and limiting thoughts and replaced them with positive thoughts and limitless beliefs.

I relinquished self-criticism and replaced it with self-compassion, and I started to approach myself with kindness and understanding. When confronted with personal failings, honoring and accepting my humanness comprised of self-compassion, mindfulness, courage, self-respect, and surrender. I actively live life in accordance with those values, transforming negative thought habits, attitudes, and emotional biases into positive ones. Self-compassion is essential for our overall mind, body, and soul's well-being. We spend more time with ourselves than anyone else, and how we relate to ourselves has a significant impact on how we feel. I started to cultivate a great respect for myself and expressed gratitude for my body and mind. I began to look at myself with admiration for what I saw.

Judging my mind was easy. *You are so slow, how stupid were you?* Looking at my body, I used to criticize it for whatever reason: too fat, too thin, too short, too tall, too much cellulite. The list goes on. When I reflected, I realized this brilliant, intelligent body knew exactly what to give me when I needed it. When I had to fight for my life, this body gave me the strength to fight. When it was necessary, it presented as dead, and when I was going through cancer treatment, it knew to retain water to have me expand beyond my usual size to minimize the cast-off of the radiation to my organs. Looking at my mind and body through the lens of self-compassion and understanding shifted my perspective. This was not a body that I wanted to dishonor. This is a body and mind I wanted to love for all it had given me in this life. This change in behavior to increase self-compassion has genuinely benefited my body, mind, and soul.

I relinquished doubt and welcomed self-worth. Knowing my worth was a big lesson, and it started with the willingness to accept that I am worthy. Through therapy and self-love coaching, I cultivated my worth of love, happiness, joy, and so much more. Over time, I had to change the way I was doing things in my life, be intentional with the interactions I allowed, and learn to set boundaries. This improved my self-worth tremendously, thereby improving my overall well-being. Self-love through self-love coaching goes way beyond self-care. Self-love is about accepting *every* aspect of yourself, even those parts you've learned to suppress or hide.

According to an article from the Berkeley Well-Being Institute, the thing about low self-esteem is we accidentally create the exact situations we need to avoid in order to boost self-esteem. According to the article, studies found participants with low self-esteem tended to choose a report with a negative self-evaluation over a positive self-evaluation. This research suggests that if we have low self-esteem, we often put ourselves in situations that keep our self-esteem low. For example, we may choose a romantic partner who puts us down, a job that underappreciates us, or friends who belittle us. Practicing self-love restores our self-worth.

I started taking stock of the people and situations I exposed myself to, protecting my energy by surrounding myself with positive people who held space for me, and setting clear boundaries. I started to focus on solutions rather than problems. I don't try to fix things for others, and I have learned to respond instead of react in difficult situations. I have learned to set clear boundaries with the people in my life, and I learned to put myself first. As the saying goes, you cannot pour from an empty cup.

By doing so, I started recognizing the ways my self-esteem stayed low and started putting myself in more situations in which people supported and loved me unconditionally. Now, I wake up in the morning and know I am enough just as I am. I go to bed at night and know I am enough and am deserving of a joyful and peaceful life despite the ups and downs. I've learned if someone does not think you are worthy or enough, it is their opinion of you, and you do not have to take it on as your truth. Your truth exists within you, and the fact you exist in this life and dare to live an authentic life means you are enough and worthy of only the best. Knowing my worth came with the understanding and acknowledgment I am human and flawed.

I relinquished the need to control and welcomed faith. I bought myself a butterfly-shaped key ring that read, "Now faith is the substance of things hoped for, the evidence of things not seen, Hebrews 11:1." We are the coauthors of our lives, and we must allow the universe to cocreate with us. When we know there is a Higher Power at work for our greater good, we can trust in Divine Goodness. When we're attached to outcomes in our lives, it quickly leads to suffering and pain. Once we can detach from trying to control and plan life, we're no longer blocked but instead open to receiving life's magical moments.

I relinquished disconnectedness and welcomed the connectedness of self. Through self-love coaching, I found connecting with myself through mirror work has been transformational. At first, mirror work can be intimidating because not everybody likes to look at themselves in a mirror. However, I have found it is an essential part of my day to acknowledge the person in the mirror. Most people look in a mirror only to criticize what they see, but I have come to recognize the beautiful, kind, compassionate, and inspirational person who stares back at me. I take the time in the mirror to practice positive affirmations, express gratitude, and check in with myself. I take the opportunity to do mirror work to be kind and supportive, which has helped me connect to myself. I encourage you to love the self in the mirror and let that time become a pleasure to spend time with yourself.

I relinquished being confined to shelter and welcomed being present in nature. When I spend time in nature, I am reminded of the words of Sadhguru. He said trees are our closest relatives. What they exhale, we inhale; what we exhale, they inhale. Trees keep our lives going, just like the outer part of our lungs. You cannot ignore your body if you want to live, and the planet is in no way different from this. What you call "my body" is just a piece of this planet. And the very essence of the spiritual process is about just this. This comparison made me feel happy and connected to Mother Earth and it bestowed upon me a sense of peace.

According to a *Frontiers in Psychology* article, two types of human-nature interactions can impact one's inner peace and happiness levels. Based on thirty samples, a fixed-effect meta-analysis found that those who were more connected to nature tended to experience more positive effects, vitality, and life satisfaction compared to those less connected to nature. Vitality had the strongest relationship with nature connectedness, followed by positive effect and life satisfaction. With the odds of improving overall vitality looking good to improve my overall happiness and vitality, I started to incorporate regular nature walks and social activities in nature into my routine. The results suggest that closer human-nature relationships do not have to come at the expense of happiness. Rather, this meta-analysis showed being connected to nature and feeling happy are, in fact, connected.

I relinquished the past and welcomed the present. Many of us get stuck in the past because we have a need for certainty. We are creatures of survival, so we are hard-wired to have some amount of certainty in our lives. I needed to feel certain I could avoid pain and, ideally, find some comfort in my life. I realized I was not experiencing life in the present; I was experiencing my mind. Through my thoughts, I kept the past alive in my daily conversations. When I acknowledged that, I realized I was responding in the present from a place in the past, which was a barrier to the authenticity I sought. With the help of my psychologist, we found a way for me to find a place in my past for all the memories to live. Once I achieved that, I found I was no longer bothered or triggered by memories of the past in the present. This made it easier to live in the present moment.

I learned to let go of the past, and that meant stepping into the unknown. It meant having the courage to let go of what is familiar, even if it was negative, and being vulnerable enough to embrace and learn from the present and what lay ahead.

In order for me to welcome my authentic self, I had to let go of the idealistic self. That meant all the changes I once thought of as devastating and humiliating was necessary in order to usher in the new. Stepping into my authentic self has allowed for true empowerment. I encourage you to step into your authentic life, into the unique particular being you are.

CHAPTER TEN:

STEPPING OUT OF TRAUMA

"The beauty of the soul; inner peace and joy."
—LAILAH GIFTY AKITA

In Chapter One, I start with a quote by Peter A. Levine that says, "Trauma is a fact of life. It does not, however, have to be a life sentence." This statement is so powerful, yet as a survivor of traumatic experiences, I can tell you that I made trauma a life sentence for the longest time in a small prison with high walls and very little light. In doing so, I robbed myself of the true moments of joy, the sense of inner peace, and the freedom to live my life to the fullest. I was in desperate need of finding the light.

Throughout life, we are presented by opportunities to choose—some big, some small—like meeting someone new, falling in love, becoming a new parent, losing a parent, experiencing great financial rewards and recognition, losing a job, experiencing great health, or being diagnosed with a dreaded disease. I could carry on, but in my experience these are all opportunities life brings us to evaluate our lives and make choices.

If you abuse alcohol and are diagnosed with sclerosis of the liver, that is an opportunity life presents for you to stop abusing alcohol and reevaluate your life. If you are like me and you always reach for relationships with partners who create dependency, ask yourself what life is trying to show you. It usually starts with a partner who suffers from low self-worth and does not believe they are enough to sustain a relationship with an empowered partner. So instead of stepping up and being the partner required in a balanced, empowered relationship, they create a dependency so they can feel secure in the relationship knowing the partner won't leave them. When this happens, I ask myself, "What it is about me that lands me in the same situation with a different person time after time?"

Life presented me with many opportunities to let go of this self-inflicted life sentence and break down the prison walls, but I chose not to because it was hard to from the depths of despair. At first, life was nudging me along, and eventually it hit me head on. It presented me with the wake-up call, another trauma, a diagnosis of a dreaded disease. Only then did I pay attention.

I am telling you this because I want you to know you have the power within to free yourself. Don't wait for life to make the decision for you. I know it is difficult to undertake this daunting task when we are in the depths of despair and we feel sadness, anger, resentment, fear, and guilt, but I know true healing starts with connection. At the beginning of the book, I say "talk about it," and that means make the decision and start. Reach out to a professional psychologist, a therapist, a support group, or a close ally like a best friend. One of the most powerful lessons I learned that changed my life was the power of speaking to survivors. There is a strong connection because there is a shared ability to understand and get each other on a level no one else can.

This took me back to a fundraiser I attended many years ago. The guest speaker at the function was a fellow survivor. Her story of survival was riveting, and as much as I experienced chills for the violent rape and murder attack on her life, I was inspired by her standing in front of a crowded room sharing her story in such an impactful and moving way. When everyone was enjoying the delicious luncheon, I sneaked out to have a private conversation with her. She told me many women just like me share their experiences with her following her many speaking engagements. The majority shared with her that they kept their traumatic experiences to themselves, not telling their spouses, parents, siblings, and friends, but chose to only share with her because she was a survivor.

It was the first time in my life I was sharing with someone who could understand me in a way that nobody else could. The power of that discussion with a fellow survivor changed my life. I remember going to therapy and asking, "What happened?" It turns out speaking to a fellow survivor helped me to apply the compassion I shared with her freely to myself. I also gained a different perspective on how I viewed my experiences, and it helped me unlock the courage to take the step toward freedom, joy, and inner peace.

According to Dr. Gabor Maté, trauma is not what happens to you, it's what happens inside you as a result of what happened to you. Trauma is just the beginning, and when we start the healing journey, it is important to take a holistic approach to healing, focusing on the mind, body, and spirit. I wish to share some of my lessons with you.

When we experience trauma, we lose our body and our sense of self. Our senses become muffled, and we no longer feel alive. According to Bessel van der Kolk, trauma victims cannot recover until they become familiar with and befriend the sensations of their bodies. Being frightened means you live in a body that is always on guard. Angry people live in angry bodies. The bodies of child abuse victims are tense and defensive until they find a way to relax and feel safe. Van der Kolk suggested in order to change, people need to become aware of their sensations and the way their bodies interact with the world around them. Physical self-awareness is the first step in releasing the tyranny of the past.

Stepping out of my trauma started with the acknowledgment that something bad had happened to me and the willingness to heal from the trauma. With professional help, I began processing sensations and emotions, describing and identifying my feelings and how I felt in my body when I had the experiences. This was necessary to reconnect with my body and mind. According to van der Kolk, the most natural way for human beings to calm themselves down is by clinging to another person. This means it is a challenge for survivors like me who have been physically and sexually violated to enjoy physical touch. With the help of therapy with a sexologist and psychotherapy with a psychologist, I retrained my mind to feel physical sensations and my body to enjoy the comforts of physical touch. At the same time, I learned to remember what happened and integrate the memories as belonging to the past.

Once my mind and my body were connected, they could reconnect to the self with greater self-awareness. This meant I could be free to have memories and feel my feelings and emotions without becoming overwhelmed, enraged, or withdrawn. This meant I was no longer keeping secrets; I opened up about my trauma experiences; I found a way to be fully alive and not sleepwalk through my life; I could experience smells, sounds, and images from the past without being disturbed.

Reaching this level of connection with the self was a true breakthrough for me, and when I reached that point, I realized there is no such thing as mind and body without spirit. This led me down the path of mindfulness, which is at the very core of self-awareness. I started expanding on my already developed mind and body connection, and with the help of self-development work, I engaged in a greater awareness between my thoughts and my physical sensations. I allowed myself to feel during a breakup in a romantic relationship; I would allow myself to feel the pain and the disappointment and work through it in order to release the feelings from a place of love. This helped substantially in managing triggers, because once the feelings and emotions were effectively processed and released, it could no longer harm me.

I spoke about my family, friends, support groups, and my best friend throughout the book. They are all part of my support system, and they play a great role in making me feel safe and loved. It is a safe space where there is no shame, no judgment, only love and encouragement. People who are supposed to love you should never hurt you. As part of my healing, I make a conscious decision to spend time with the people in my support network. Whether it is spending time with family at the beach, having lunch with my best friend, catching up over coffee, talking on the cell phone, or popping into a support group, I am intentional with my connections. Bessel van der Kolk said, "Our attachment bonds are our greatest protection against threat."

At a support group and on the journey to write this book, I discovered healing takes place in community. Through connection and collaboration, we are able to share and heal together. At a group session I attended, one of the members had passed away since the last meeting. The connection between the survivors was strong, because even though there was a heaviness about the passing of a friend, we all joined in remembering and sharing positive memories which lifted our spirits. Before long, we could crack a smile, and we could allow ourselves to feel sad, content, and fortunate at the same time.

I learned to overcome the stigma associated with medication. When doctors prescribed medication for anxiety after my cancer diagnosis, I came home and chucked it in the medicine cabinet. Despite experiencing severe anxiety while going through cancer treatment, I believed I could cope on my own. It had been years since I had prescription medication to help cope mentally. In meeting with my spiritual medium, I was connected with my angels and spirit guides. They are a team

I have worked with for most of my life. To my horror, they reminded me medication had a purpose and that I needed to take the medication that I got from the pharmacy, which, according to them, I was not taking. This made me giggle, because I realized we are never alone. This was confirmation, needless to say, so I went home and took the medication. It was the best decision I made because the medication is part of holistic treatment following trauma, and we should not be discouraged because of the stigma associated with medication for mental health.

I also learned on the healing journey that negative and positive emotions can coexist because we don't heal in silos, and it was an important lesson to learn because sometimes we feel guilty if we smile following trauma. When we experience the death of a loved one, it almost feels wrong to laugh. Following my attack, it felt like sadness and anger was the order of the day because of the extent and the violent nature of the trauma, so laughter felt almost out of place. I had to learn it was okay to allow myself to feel both positive and negative emotions at the same time. For example, it was okay to be sad in one moment and then happy. It was okay to allow myself to laugh even when I was sad. So, give yourself permission to feel both.

Once I reached this level on my healing journey, I was able to better self-regulate, and I was able to experience life the way it was always meant to be lived. Early on in my healing process, I was able to experience posttraumatic growth with the need to give back and volunteer in an ambulance. During my time as a volunteer, I wanted to be the "blue eyes," the ray of light for someone else, sharing safety and hope, providing the assurance the person I was looking at was okay. Throughout my life, I held the belief that we were rays of light for our Higher Power. I remember singing a song in Sunday school about being a ray of light for Jesus and feeling honored to be chosen. Our Sunday school teacher handed us this paper cutout of a happy face that had a ray of light all around its head. On the edge of the top of the head, it read, "*Sonstraaltjies vir Jesus*," meaning a ray of light for Jesus. I still keep my ray of light cutout because it serves as a reminder of how special we are as human beings and that we have the light within us. When things in life are good, it is easy to find our light and see the light in others. However, when life hands us the worst experiences and darkest times of despair, we can forget we have this little light in us that brings us hope, but the good news is there is always someone else who will shine their light so we can see in the dark.

This reminds me of the time I was sitting in the hospital hallway with my best friend after receiving the cancer diagnosis. Her being there, holding space for me, and loving and supporting me was how she shined her light when I forgot I had one. My family and friends showed me compassion, love, and unconditional support, and that was their way of shining their light so I could find hope. I received much light from others during my life in the most unexpected places. I remember checking in at the hospital for my second surgery and the administrator that was handling the registration said there were two ladies who were waiting for me in the ward. I was surprised because I was not expecting anyone. When I got to the ward, it was a friend from university and her colleague who had heard about my diagnosis and the treatment. They came to the hospital that day to let me know

I was not alone, to wish me well, and to say a prayer with me ahead of the surgery. My heart was full, and I experienced so much love, compassion, gratitude, joy, and peace in that moment. They were shining their ray of light for me to find hope. That feeling of honor I felt as a child to be this ray of light and to be among other rays of light still existed in me and was stronger than ever, and the evidence was everywhere. We all have the ability to be the ray of light in our own lives and the lives of others. Sometimes that is all it takes to gift someone hope, a moment of joy, and inner peace.

This theme of the ray of light tied in closely with the posttraumatic growth I experienced. According to the July 2015 article "How trauma can change you for the better" in *Time*, 50 percent of trauma survivors experience posttraumatic growth following a traumatic event. At first, my posttraumatic growth started with my willingness to embrace change, make a difference, and do the work, which I did many years' worth of. Once I did, I experienced growth in personal strength, I found a new appreciation for life, new possibilities in life, religious and spiritual change, and improved relationships with others. Even starting my podcast and writing this book are signs of my posttraumatic growth and shining my light for others and sharing hope. Through the posttraumatic growth experience, I could harness my ability to be the ray of light in my life and also in the lives of others. Living life from this centered place that exudes light was so much better, and I felt in touch with the flow and the purpose of my life. I continue to find ways to take new meaning from my experiences to live my life in a more meaningful way than prior to the trauma. Experiencing life in this way fills me with happiness.

According to a Lumen course on finding happiness, some psychologists have suggested happiness consists of three distinct elements: the pleasant life, the good life, and the meaningful life. A pleasant life is realized through the attainment of day-to-day pleasures that add fun, joy, and excitement to our lives. For example, evening walks along the beach and a fulfilling sex life can enhance our daily pleasure and contribute to a pleasant life. Psychologists suggested the good life is achieved through identifying our unique skills and abilities and engaging these talents to enrich our lives; those who achieve the good life often find themselves absorbed in their work or their recreational pursuits. The meaningful life involves a deep sense of fulfillment that comes from using our talents in the service of the greater good: in ways that benefit the lives of others or make the world a better place. They said, in general, the happiest people tend to be those who pursue the full life, the ones who orient their pursuits toward all three elements. This was exactly what happiness looked like to me, but I still craved joy and inner peace.

I was happy but I missed the moments of joy that bring one to a place of knowing that all is well, so I looked into joy. Brooklyn-based designer and writer Ingrid Fetell Lee described joy in her TED talk as being much simpler than happiness and more immediate. According to Ingrid, the way psychologists define joy is as an intense, momentary experience of positive emotion. We can measure that through direct physical expressions, like smiling and laughing or feeling the need to jump up in the air. Ingrid said there's something that happens physically viscerally in our bodies when we feel joy.

She suggested happiness can sometimes feel a little bit vague. It's hard to know in a given moment how happy we are; it requires some self-reflection. It is much more immediate when we are experiencing a moment of joy. There's no doubt. In her opinion, we overlook this because these moments of joy often seem so small; they sort of pass by in the flow of daily life. So we don't often pay a lot of attention to them. They don't really feel like they're very important. And yet, they're really important and powerful.

According to Ingrid, research shows we make more accurate decisions when we're in a joyful state of mind, and we consider a broader range of scenarios in the process of making those decisions. Some research shows we're up to 12 percent more productive in a state of joy. Joy also opens us up to new ideas, and joy makes us more resilient. Small moments of joy can counteract the physical effects of stress, like elevated blood pressure and heart rate. Moments of joy bring those measures down and help the body recover from the effects of stress. So, when we get stressed out about anything, we don't have time for joy or for play or for fun. Now, we may need to focus to get things done. But in fact, those little moments of joy actually improve our emotional resilience, especially when we're dealing with difficult times.

I love the fact that when we experience joy, there is no doubt and it is immediate. I recently experienced this moment of joy when my niece and her husband brought me a cake box. I was so excited to open this box and tucked into it a delicious cupcake! To my absolute surprise, I found a baby outfit, tiny shoes for tiny feet, and a positive pregnancy test. That moment of joy filled my heart immediately; there was no doubt I was experiencing joy, and it manifested as Ingrid had said in a physical expression of tears of joy. When I find those moments, I experience them as they unfold, and I savor them. I am intentional about taking a pause in those moments, and interestingly enough, they complement the inner peace my new way of life brings me. Dr. Wayne Dyer said, "Inner peace is the result of retraining your mind to process life as it is, rather than as you think it should be."

This quote speaks volumes, because I have found peace living in the present moment, not reaching for the past, and not living in the what-ifs of the future. This takes me back to my parent's grief when mourning the loss of my brother. When they lost their son, a part of them stayed in the past and repeated the events and the search for answers. This carried on for years, and because they were sad and in pain, they could not allow themselves to find joy or have inner peace. They were always haunted by the events of that night. Not until my parents changed their perception of the situation did they accept we were not going to have the answers to what happened to my brother. He was never coming back. My parents accepted they could not change the past, they accepted they were not going to have answers, and instead of living in the past, they started celebrating by brother in the present. This shift allowed them to celebrate my brother's life and know he would always live on through his widow and his kids. Our family will honor his legacy and memory, as is, in the present moment. My parents were free from their past trauma experience and open to experiencing life the way it is, rather than the way they thought it should be. Now, when we celebrate my brother, we do so not from a place of sadness and sorrow but from the centered place of joy and inner peace.

Stepping out of trauma is a choice that starts with the willingness to change, and doing the work required to live a life of meaning and purpose. In our purpose, we find our freedom, and in freedom we find joy and inner peace. My life has not been moonshine and roses, and the healing journey has by no means been perfect, but I discovered a purposeful life, free of trauma, filled with rays of light, joy, and inner peace.

ACKNOWLEDGMENTS

Thank you to everyone who has been a part of my journey to write *Ray of Light*. There is no way such a blessing would have been realized without your encouragement, guidance, and care for my life's calling.

I'd like to start by thanking my family for walking by my side in this journey of life, every step of the way, from the moment I fell in love with stories and storytelling to the grueling task of revising my whole manuscript. I'm grateful for my dad, my mom, my three brothers, my two sisters, my niece, her husband, and my two best friends for providing me with the deep emotional support I needed to see this journey through. Without their daily support from the beginning, I would never have felt comfortable dreaming a dream so wild as being an author.

Daddy, you are my biggest fan. I'm forever grateful to my dad, who is my dearest friend. On the days when I needed someone to talk ideas through and when my hope of being a writer was held together by a precarious thread, my dad would stitch this thread to a sturdy piece of cloth every time.

Thank you to my mom for inspiring my love of language, stories, and storytelling. You'll always be my favorite storyteller through your beautiful poetry. I'm grateful to you for teaching me everything about the importance of language and reading from a young age.

I'm thankful for my brothers and my sisters, who push me to be better than I think I can be. Thank you for being my soundboard and for encouraging my dreams. You guys remind me to dream big and to always remain close to God.

I am thankful to my two best friends who are my greatest confidants in my writing and in life. They encouraged me to steadily keep going, especially on the days when I wanted to give up or suffer from imposter syndrome. Thank you for listening to my ridiculous ramblings, worries, and zany writing ideas without judgment. You not only appreciate my weirdness, but you welcome it.

Thank you to my niece for your unconditional support, starting with the night you hugged me in the back of the car at six years old and said, "It's okay," to popping by to keep me company during revisions. You are my treasure.

Secondly, I'd like to thank all the people whose stories I share in my book. Your bravery in being vulnerable with me has been very inspiring. Thank you for trusting me to tell your stories with the care and compassion you deserve. You are all my heroes.

Primary Interviews

- Rosalind Pistilli
- Anissa Tolliver
- Robyn Russell
- CarmenMaria Navarro
- Robynette Lila Dhari
- Laura Zam

Secondary Interviews

- Ingrid Fetell Lee
- Laura Thomas
- Greg Tolkinson
- Sarah Montana
- Stacey Kramer

Next, I'd like to thank Eric Koester. You believed in me and my writing since day one of this project. I will never forget waiting for you to call so I could pitch my book idea to you. I thought to myself, *I have lost so much already, what have I got to lose?* When you called, I went for it. I'm forever grateful for your unconditional support and belief that I have the potential to become a published author.

I'd also like to thank Asa Loevenstein, Brian Bies, Bojana Gigovska, ChandaElaine Spurlock, Christy Mossburg, Gjorgji Pejkovski, Heather Gomez, Hayley Newlin, Jordan Waterwash, Mackenzie Joyce, Mateusz Cichosz, Natalie Bailey, Sherman Morrison, Simona Gjurovska, Stacey Hickman, Venus Bradley, and the incredible team I've had the honor to work with at the Creator Institute and New Degree Press. You've all given me the thrill of a lifetime. Thank you for making my dream of sharing my story with the world come true.

I would also like to extend a huge thank-you to my marketing and revisions editor, Rebecca Bruckenstein. Thank you for guarding my vision for this book and working with me on my chapters to realize this vision. Thank you for letting me access your incredible mind to help me transform this manuscript into something I am proud of. You have been instrumental in bringing this vision to life, and every day I am grateful to have you with me on this amazing journey. I truly appreciate your pushing me to dig deeper to tell the story that needed to be heard and constantly guiding me to become the best author I can be. You enriched my life in so many ways, and I have learned and grown so much with you. I will always cherish and think fondly of our Sunday night catch-ups, giggles, and many powerful conversations.

Finally, thank you to everyone and anyone who believes in me and my writing. You are my constant stars in the vast night sky shining and encouraging me to keep writing. Thank you very much to everyone who provided feedback on early drafts of my manuscript. I'm so grateful for your help to make this book the best it can be. A special thank you to everyone who preordered a copy of my book and donated to my prelaunch campaign. Thank you very much for reminding me there are so many people in my communities who love and care about me.

Grace Lunika, Warda Steyn, Guillermo Erasmus, Lanaine Abrahams, Payton Lynch, CarmenMaria Navarro, Carol Yee, Jennifer Tam, Louis McLaren, Eric Koester, Maxene January, Yujin Kim, Alexis Young, Nils Junge, Serena Hu, Precious McKoy, Adela Fortune, Sylvester Jenkins III, Lamise Inglis, David McConnell, Cornelius January, Marlena Jbara, Cézanne Britain, Doris Sew Hoy, Robyn Russell, Jennifer Rose Asher, Ameer Steyn, Zaahra Steyn, Salma Steyn, Momma T, Andrew McConnell, Carla Ahrends, Ronnellie Esterhuizen, Kayley James, Elisabeth Blomqvist, Ntlhobogi Thaanyane, Nurjahan Khatun, Melody Makeka, Elli Waldrop, Valeria Aloe, Keith Doley, Gareth Hawkey, Ethan Bacus, Andrew Theunissen, Laura Smyth, Graham Dreyden, "Peanut" James, Matthew Unger, and Lucille Jenneker.

APPENDIX

CHAPTER ONE

American Psychological Association. "Trauma." Accessed October 8, 2021 https://www.apa.org/topics/trauma.

Janoff-Bulman, R. *Shattered Assumptions: Towards a New Psychology of Trauma.* New York: The Free Press. 1992.

Kleber, Rolf J. "Trauma and Public Mental Health: A Focused Review." *Frontiers in Psychiatry.* June 25, 2019. https://doi.org/10.3389/fpsyt.2019.00451.

Pistilli, Rosalind. "Interview - Rosalind Pistilli." Interview by Marlene McConnell. May 12, 2021. Audio, 02:20 https://www.buzzsprout.com/1539454.

Tedeschi, Richard G. and Lawrence G. Calhoun. "Growth: Conceptual Foundations and Empirical Evidence" *Psychological Inquiry.* vol. 15. No 1. (2004) 1-18 https://www.jstor.org/stable/20447194.

Snyder, C R. *Coping: The Psychology of What Works.* New York: Oxford University Press. 1999.

Rendon, Jim. "How trauma can change you for the better." *Time.* July 22, 2015 Accessed October 2, 2021 https://time.com/3967885/how-trauma-can-change-you-for-the-better/.

Rubner, Justin B. "Professor Survives Airplane Crash." *The Red & Black*, November 1, 2000. https://www.redandblack.com/news/professor-survives-airplane-crash/article_6afae18c-5ce8-5ba8-a19c-c35ba21d0a57.html.

CHAPTER TWO

American Psychiatric Association . "What is Psychotherapy" *American Psychiatry Association*. Accessed October 9, 2021. https://www.psychiatry.org/patients-families/psychotherapy.

American Psychological Association. "Understanding Psychotherapy and How It Works." Last modified July 31, 2020. http://www.apa.org/helpcenter/understanding-psychotherapy.aspx.

Kantor, Viktoria, Matthias Knefel, and Brigette Leuger-Shuster. "Perceived Barriers and Facilitators of Mental Health Service Utilization in Adult Trauma Survivors: A Systematic Review." *Clinical Psychological Review*, vol. 52 (March 2017): 52-68 https://www.sciencedirect.com/science/article/pii/S0272735816303373.

Karlsson, H. How Psychotherapy changes the Brain. *Psychiatric Times*. 2011. https://www.psychiatry.org/patients-families/psychotherapy.

CHAPTER THREE

Ludwig, Petr. "Decision Paralysis: How to Stop Overthinking Your Choices." Procrastination(Blog). Accessed January 18, 2022. https://procrastination.com/blog/9/decision-paralysis-overthinking-choices.

PsychCentral. "What are the Signs of Codependency." *PsychCentral*. June 10,2021. https://psychcentral.com/lib/symptoms-signs-of-codependency.

CHAPTER FOUR

Alter, Cathy. " 'Pandemic grief' Proves Especially Devastating and Complex for Many in Mourning , Health Experts Say". *Washington Post.* March 28, 2021. https://www.washingtonpost.com/health/pandemic-grief-lasting-bereavement/2021/03/26/18ce5878-8be8-11eb-9423-04079921c915_story.html.

American Psychological Association. "Grieving Life and Loss: The Pandemic has Led to a Series of Losses, from Financial Security to the Lives of Loved Ones. How Can We Heal?." Accessed October 10, 2021. https://www.apa.org/monitor/2020/06/covid-grieving-life.

Larkin, Alexandra. "Ramifications of South Africa's Dop System". *South African History Online.* Accessed January 22, 2022. https://www.sahistory.org.za/article/ramifications-south-africas-dop-system-alexandra-larkin.

Long, Gerard. "Interview - Gerard Long". Interview by Marlene McConnell. December 1, 2021. Audio, 15:26 https://www.buzzsprout.com/1539454.

Parkes, Colin Murray. "Coping with Loss: Bereavement in Adult Life". *The BMJ.*(1998). https://doi.org/10.1136/bmj.316.7134.856.

Shear, M. Katherine. "Grief and Mourning Gone Awry: Pathway and Course of Complicated Grief." *Dialogues in Clinical Neuroscience.* vol. 14 no. 2(June 2012): 119-228. https://www.ncbi.nlm.nih.gov/pmc/articles/PMC3384440/.

South African Government. "History". Accessed January 22, 2022. https://www.gov.za/about-sa/history.

Thomas, Laura. "Navigating the World of Grief". Filmed December 2019 at TEDxCherry/creekWomen, an independent event. TED video, 12:37. https://www.ted.com/talks/laura_thomas_navigating_the_world_of_grief.

Tyrrell, Patrick, Seneca Harberger, and Waquar Siddiqui. "Stages of Dying". *National Center for Biotechnology Information, U.S. National Library of Medicine.* April 6, 2021. https://www.ncbi.nlm.nih.gov/books/NBK507885/.

CHAPTER FIVE

Healthline. "What is Ayahuasca? Experience, Benefits and Side Effects." Accessed January 25, 2022. https://www.healthline.com/nutrition/ayahuasca.

Koening, Harold G. "Religion, Spirituality, and Health: The Research and Clinical Implication" *International Scholarly Research Notices.* vol. 2012(2012).https://doi.org/10.5402/2012/278730.

Leigh's Mission. "Our Story". Accessed January 24, 2022, https://leighsmission.com/.

Multidisciplinary Association for Psychedelic Studies. "The Ayehuasca Phenomenom". Accessed January 25, 2022, https://maps.org/2014/11/20/the-ayahuasca-phenomenon/.

Peres, Julio F.P., Alexander Moreira-Almeida, Antonia Gladys Nasello, and Harold G.Koening. "Spirituality and Resilience in Trauma Victims". *Journal of Religion and Health.* vol.46 no.3 (2007):343-350. https://www.researchgate.net/publication/226642926_Spirituality_and_Resilience_in_Trauma_Victims.

PsychCentral. "11 ways to Cultivate Resilience." *PsychCentral.* Accessed October 8, 2021, https://psychcentral.com/lib/11-ways-to-cultivate-resilience#5.

Harris, Maxine, and Landis, Christine. *Sexual Abuse in the Lives of Women Diagnosed with Serious Mental Illness.* 346. Amsterdam; Harwood Academic Publishers, 1997.https://books.google.co.za/books?hl=en&lr=&id=XxfPCwAAQBAJ&oi=fnd&pg=PA337&dq=spirituality+and+trauma&ots=65yM-EU-

GVc&sig=yn5-9qEVnQs81dQh2tl5jzzhsR8#v=onepage&q=spirituality%20and%20trauma&f=false.

TED. "Greg Tolkinson: Faith and Doubt" April 12, 2017. Video 15:30. https://www.youtube.com/watch?v=ALafX-xH11c.

The Art of Living. "The Inimitable Connection Between Dandiya, Garba and Navratri!". Art of Living. Accessed March 1, 2022. https://www.artofliving.org/navratri/inimitable-connection-dandiya-garba-navratri.

Williams, Monnica "Introducing Ayahuasca". *Psychology Today*. Accessed January 25, 2022, https://www.psychologytoday.com/za/blog/culturally-speaking/201912/introducing-ayahuasca.

CHAPTER SIX

Greater Good Magazine. "What is Forgiveness." Accessed October 11, 2021. https://greatergood.berkeley.edu/topic/forgiveness/definition.

Lichtenfelt, Stephanie, Maier, Markus A., Buechner, Vanessa L., Capo, and Maria Fernandez. "The Influence of Decisional and Emotional Forgiveness on Attributions." *Frontiers in Psychology*. June 25, 2019 https://www.ncbi.nlm.nih.gov/pmc/articles/PMC6603330/.

Montana, Sarah. "The Real Risk of Forgiveness and Why it's Worth It." Filmed March 2018 at TedxLincolnSquare, Video 15:53. https://www.ted.com/talks/sarah_montana_why_forgiveness_is_worth_it?language=en.

Sarah Montana. "about." Accessed October 11, 2021. https://www.sarahmontana.com/about-full.

CHAPTER SEVEN

Kramer, Stacey. "The Best Gift I Ever Survived." Filmed at TED2010, Video 03:01. https://www.ted.com/talks/stacey_kramer_the_

best_gift_i_ever_survived?utm_campaign=tedspread&utm_medium=referral&utm_source=tedcomshare.

Stanbourough, Rebecca Joy. "What is Vibrational Energy". *Healthline*. November 13, 2020. https://www.healthline.com/health/vibrational-energy#change-your-vibrational-energy.

CHAPTER EIGHT

Deliramich, Aimee N. and Matt J Gray. "Changes in Women's Sexual Behaviour Following Sexual Assault." *Behavior Modification*, vol. 32 no.5(2008): 611-621. doi:10.1177/0145445508314642.

Prabha, PV Gouri, and Shruti Lekha. "Child Sexual Abuse: A Stigma for Society." *IJ Rar*, vol. 7. no. 3(September 2020):49-52. https://www.researchgate.net/publication/344250025_Child_Sexual_Abuse_A_Stigma_for_Society.

World Health Organization. "Violence Against Children." Accessed January 22, 2022. https://www.who.int/news-room/fact-sheets/detail/violence-against-children.

CHAPTER NINE

Berkley Wellbeing Institute. "Knowing Your Worth: How to Boost Self-worth and Self-confidence." Accessed October 10, 2021. https://www.berkeleywellbeing.com/knowing-your-worth.html.

Brown, Brene. "Listening to Shame" Filmed at TED2012. Video, 20:22. https://www.ted.com/talks/brene_brown_listening_to_shame?language=en.

Capaldi, Colin A., Raelyne L. Dopko, and John M. Zelenski. "The Relationship Between Nature Connectedness and Happiness: a Meta-Analysis" *Frontiers in Psychology*. September 8, 2014. https://www.frontiersin.org/articles/10.3389/fpsyg.2014.00976/full.

TED. "Dr. Maria Sirois: Living an Authentic Life" January 14, 2013. Video 14:36. https://www.youtube.com/watch?v=ohGMg-LJCjs .

Isha. "Trees, Our Closet Relatives" November 1, 2017. https://isha.sadhguru.org/global/en/sadhguru/man/trees-closest-relative.

CHAPTER TEN

Harvard Health Publishing. "Giving Thanks Can Make You Happier." Accessed February 2, 2022. https://www.health.harvard.edu/healthbeat/giving-thanks-can-make-you-happier.

TED. "Ingrid Fetell Lee: Why We Pursue Happiness But Overlook Joy" January 14, 2019. Video 6:58. https://www.youtube.com/watch?v=V_tMeSgw_DM .Levine, Peter. *Waking the Tiger: Healing Trauma*. Berkley, CA: North Atlantic Books, 1997.

Lumen Introduction to Psychology. "The Pursuit of Happiness." Accessed February 2, 2022 https://courses.lumenlearning.com/atd-bhcc-intropsych/chapter/the-pursuit-of-happiness/.

van der Kolk, Bessel. *The Body Keeps the Score. Mind, Brain and Body in the Transformation of Trauma*. New York, NY: Penguin Books.2014.

WuXiaoli, Atipatsa CKaminga,DaiWenjie, DengJing, Wang-Zhipeng, PanXiongfeng, and LiuAizhong. "The prevalence of moderate-to-high posttraumatic growth: A Systematic Review and Meta-analysis." *Journal of Affective Disorders*. vol 15 no. 243(Jaunary 2019): 408-415. doi: 10.1016/j.jad.2018.09.023.

www.ingramcontent.com/pod-product-compliance
Lightning Source LLC
LaVergne TN
LVHW012020060526
838201LV00061B/4388